The Origin of the Mosque of Cordoba

The Origin of the Mosque of Cordoba

◆

Secrets of Andalusia

Marvin H. Mills

iUniverse, Inc.
New York Lincoln Shanghai

The Origin of the Mosque of Cordoba
Secrets of Andalusia

Copyright © 2006 by Marvin H. Mills

All rights reserved. No part of this book may be used or reproduced by any means, graphic, electronic, or mechanical, including photocopying, recording, taping or by any information storage retrieval system without the written permission of the publisher except in the case of brief quotations embodied in critical articles and reviews.

iUniverse books may be ordered through booksellers or by contacting:

iUniverse
2021 Pine Lake Road, Suite 100
Lincoln, NE 68512
www.iuniverse.com
1-800-Authors (1-800-288-4677)

The views expressed in this work are solely those of the author and do not necessarily reflect the views of the publisher, and the publisher hereby disclaims any responsibility for them.

ISBN-13: 978-0-595-42325-5 (pbk)
ISBN-13: 978-0-595-86662-5 (ebk)
ISBN-10: 0-595-42325-6 (pbk)
ISBN-10: 0-595-86662-X (ebk)

Printed in the United States of America

Contents

List of Illustrations vii
CHAPTER 1   An Early Golden Age. 1
CHAPTER 2   Roman Antecedents. 20
CHAPTER 3   Scholarship Takes a Holiday 29
CHAPTER 4   Unity of Style 36
CHAPTER 5   Orientation and Form 39
CHAPTER 6   Astronomical Correlations 43
CHAPTER 7   Time to Construct 53
CHAPTER 8   The Lady Vanishes 56
CHAPTER 9   Heavenly Arches 60
CHAPTER 10   A Most Unusual Mihrab 70
CHAPTER 11   Gargoyles and Doves 77
CHAPTER 12   Notes from the Underground 82
CHAPTER 13   From Tower to Minaret to Belfry 85
CHAPTER 14   The Palace City of Madina Azahara 98
CHAPTER 15   The Alhambra 104
CHAPTER 16   A New Paradigm 117
Bibliography 119

List of Illustrations

Pl. Ia Carbon-14 sample source from hole in roof beam 18
Fig. Ia Mid-Points of Carbon-14 Analysis 19
Fig. VIa Kaaba astronomical diagram 51
Fig. VIb Imaginative Reconstruction 52
Pl. IXc Exterior entry on east façade 66
Fig. IXa Arch in la Casa del Citarista 67
Fig. IXb Port Diane exterior arch over doorway with alternating voussoirs 68
Fig. IXc Windows in original tower 69
Pl. Xa Mihrab front view 75
Pl. Xb Cupola in front of mihrab 76
Pl. XIa Gargoyle 79
Pl. XIb Exterior gargoyle 80
Pl. XIc Demonic bird gargoyle 81
Pl. XIIa Lower level of mosque 84
Pl. XIIIa Renaissance cover over tower 96
Fig. XIIIa Wood frame reinforcing of tower 97
Pl. XIVa Eastern Arcade Medina Azahara 103
Fig. XVa Site plan of the Alhambra 116

1

An Early Golden Age

One must step back from a detailed analysis of artifacts and buildings of Spanish Islam in order to see the sequence of development in its proper perspective. As Gilbert and Sullivan cautioned us in their light opera H.M.S. Pinafore: things are never what they seem; skim milk masquerades as cream. The mass of existing scholarship is valuable in terms of amount but not necessarily in terms of precision. A fresh look at the Mosque of Cordoba requires that we go back in time to the Phoenician era of the 2nd and 1st millennia BC and before that to a "Golden Age" stretching back thousands of years when there thrived civilizations that attained high technological and esthetic levels which eventually transmitted their influences to Spain. Hard evidence for this is minimal but circumstantial evidence is strong. Evidence and reason can explain some basic curious anomalies about the Mosque of Cordoba, as I shall try to illustrate.

The Phoenicians were not the first people to bring civilization to the Iberian peninsula when they arrived perhaps as early as the 12th century BC. There is that enigmatic phenomenon of the civilization that the ancients called Tartessos and its indigenous people the Tartessians who were there to greet the Phoenicians. While the evidence is sketchy and controversial, it seems to be the case that there was an extended period of hundreds of years when trade was carried on between the Tartessians of Andalusia in southern Iberia and the Phoenician city-states which culminated in the establishment of Phoenician port cities in Spain by the 9th century BC.

The prevalent belief that civilization began in the Near East is denied by Colin Renfrew, English archaeologist and Director of the McDonald Institute for Archaeological Research. He believes that carbon dating and bristle cone pine calibration have proven that Western Europe had an independent development as evidenced by its tomb building, metallurgy, and artifacts:

> In a single breathtaking sweep across Europe the traditional links between the early civilizations of Crete and Mycenae and the culture of early prehistoric Europe were severed.
> The Spanish tombs, for example, now dating from 3100 B.C., centuries earlier than the tombs in Crete from which they were supposed to derive! Tombs in Brittany suddenly went back to an astonishing 4000 B.C. (Colin Renfrew, *"Ancient Europe is older than we thought"*, p. 621)

He concludes:

> But what really matters is that we no longer seek to explain European prehistory by reference to the early civilizations of the eastern Mediterranean. In the right conditions, prehistoric men anywhere in the world were capable of ingenious inventions and impressive achievements. It should be the archeologist's job to study in just what economic and social conditions such things occurred. (Renfrew, p. 622)

In my view, the condition that made possible the level of eastern achievements in Western Europe was the presence of the Tartessians in settlements along the west coast of Europe whose advanced technological knowledge and high esthetic threshold enhanced the Phoenician achievements in Spain.

In what is now Lebanon was an area known by the Phoenicians themselves as Canaan before the 12th century BC and as Phoenicia after the 12th century disturbances of the Sea People. Phoenician history is shrouded in mystery concerning that sweeping movement of invading forces that changed the history of the Near East, and this mystery is at its deepest with regards to the nature of their contact with the Tartessians. While it is generally agreed that Phoenicia—that is, the Phoenician city states led by Byblos, Sidon, and Tyre—were in the advanced ranks of city states and nations of the Near East in the 12th century BC at the beginning of the

Phoenician Iron Age, the specific characteristics of the level of development of the Tartessians technologically and culturally is not clear. Who they were and where they came from is not known. But that they were once connected to an earlier, extended web of civilization seems possible.

According to the ancient sources, Cadiz, referred to then as Gadir, the Andalusian port on the Atlantic, was founded around 1104 BC but archaeological data strongly suggests the 8th century:

> At that time the Guadalquivir emptied into the ocean a little south of the present city of Seville, and it had a wide estuary whose banks were between El Rocio and Sanlucar de Barrameda. These banks, especially the eastern one, were densely inhabited by indigenous peoples of the Final Bronze age. The Guadalquivir could be navigated almost to Cordoba, and it was close to fertile agricultural zones and the mining region of Aznalcollar, where silver was mined at that time. Gadir, therefore, controlled access to the Guadalquivir and to Huelva, which was home to an indigenous population that must have dominated the mineral resources of the Riotinto region, another point of extraordinary interest for mining. The excellent strategic location of the island of Gadir was responsible for its metropolitan nature and its development as a trading center. Ships embarked from its port carrying products directed toward the Mediterranean world. In addition, Gadir was the political center which represented the Tyrian state and the other western colonies revolving around it. (Diego Ruiz Marta, The Ancient Phoenicians of the 8th and 7th Centuries B.C. in the Bay of Cadiz: State of the Research, in <u>The Phoenicians in Spain</u>, edited by M. Bierling, pp. 155-198)

Whether 12th or 9th century BC, Cadiz, the oldest city in Europe, seems to have been the link between an earlier golden age and the development of a renewed civilization in Spain. If we can believe Plato and those writers of the 19th and 20th centuries who accepted his view, there existed a large island land mass known as Atlantis which was situated somewhere in or across the Atlantic Ocean. It existed prior to the beginning of the melting of the Arctic and Antarctic ice caps sometime after the last Ice Age, about 15,000 BC, and was destroyed about 10,000 BC after various terrestrial disturbances, the most devastating resulting in the submergence of most of those lands. Atlantean scholars offer various theories as to the primary cause or causes of this massive geologic event, attributing the violent floods, earthquakes, and sinking of land masses possibly to the effect of a large piece of an exploded supernova passing close enough to the earth to exert a massive gravitational pull. This event, it is believed by some, caused the polar axis to fall to its present 23.5 degrees tilt, disturbing the climate, causing the polar ice caps to melt and resulting in the destruction of numerous species and many humans together with their advanced civilizations. The universal recollection of the great flood in the mythology of almost all peoples points, if not to this scenario, to some real cataclysmic event.

This cataclysmic theory, or some variation of it, has been carried a step further by the assumption that Tartessos was an outpost on European soil of an Atlantean civilization. The need for Atlantis to replace the lands being lost to the ocean, coupled with its ability to navigate the seas, may have encouraged the Atlanteans to move into the Asian, European, and New World areas. The concept of a mid-Atlantic advanced civilization was put forward by Plato writing in the 4th century BC in the <u>Critias</u>, <u>Timeaus</u> and <u>The Laws</u>. Due to his obvious eminence it has been difficult for subsequent scholars to discard his theory out of hand.

Some writers, offering variations on the Plato thesis, speculate that following the last Ice Age there was either or both a melting of the Arctic and Antarctic ice caps with a subsequent rise of as much as 400 feet in sea levels and disturbances of the earth's crust, perhaps aggravated by a collision with an asteroid or a near collision which caused violent earthquakes and a nuclear winter resulting in the death of most of earth's inhabitants and the extinction of various species of animals. The mastodon, saber-tooth tiger and the mammoth all disappeared about that time. This seems to be an acceptable explanation for some subsequent developments that occurred including the cataclysmic or perhaps gradual submergence of Atlantis.

Frank Joseph, a journalist and researcher, in <u>The Destruction of Atlantis</u> places the destruction of Atlantis at close to 1200 BC and locates it off the western coast of north Africa. He says it must have been about the size of Portugal, that references to its continental size by Plato are ambiguous.

The interpretations of Plato, he believes, were misleading in that they referred to standards of measurement that differed from what Plato had in mind. Since no studies of the ocean floors have found conclusive evidence of their harboring a submerged continent, he reasons that such a large size was not plausible. The Azores and the Canary Islands are remains of that civilization. He believes that Atlantis was one of several Bronze Age civilizations, its most advanced, and that its influence spread as far as Egypt. A war between Greece and Atlantis ended with the defeat of Atlantis around 1240 BC followed by a natural world calamity which destroyed their Atlantis home base in 1198 BC. The cause of the calamity, he believes, was a passing comet and accompanying meteors which devastated the earth and created a Dark Ages for the next 500 years. The comet and its meteors aggravated the sensitive Atlantic fault causing volcanoes and earthquakes.

A theory advanced by Graham Hancock, formerly a correspondent for the Economist and the London Sunday Times who became an underwater archaeologist and is now perhaps the leading proponent of an earlier golden age, in his <u>Fingerprints of the Gods</u> and <u>The Sign and the Seal</u> holds that Atlantis was not submerged but was carried by earth crust displacement towards the South Pole and subsequently, around 4000 BC, became buried by miles of ice sheets and is now known as Antarctica. According to this theory, if the ice continues to melt in our present era of global warming, as seems to be occurring, or if appropriate archaeological digs take place in Antarctica, then perhaps the civilization of Atlantis may be uncovered.

There is that intriguing map of 1513 AD, the Piri Reis map, and the Philip Bauche map of 1737 presented by Charles Hapgood in his <u>Maps of the Ancient Sea Kings</u> based ultimately on information from the time of Alexander the Great, which shows Antarctica not covered by ice. Hapgood was an American academician who died in 1982. He was one of the leading advocates of a Pole Shift theory. Albert Einstein wrote a favorable introduction to his first book, <u>The Earth's Shifting Crust</u>, in which Hapgood proposed his radical theory of sudden earth crust movements. This would mean that the region was surveyed and maps were drawn up before 4000 BC when Antarctica was still ice free. The information seems convincing in that the Piri Reis map describes fairly accurately the coastline of Antarctica that is now known to be under the ice, plus accurate identification and longitudinal placement of South America and Africa. It lead Ivar Zapp and George Erikson in Atlantis in America, 1998, to assert that an awareness of Antarctica was known to an advanced civilization that existed prior to the end of the Ice Age. Thus, ancient sailing men from an earlier time may have had the benefit of maps which adequately depicted the true geography of the earth both as an aid to and an indication of their ability to sail the vast oceans.

Colin Wilson and Rand Flem-Ath in The Atlantis Blueprint, written in 2000, base their paradigm on the Hancock supposition of earth crustal displacement which, unlike the slow concurrent displacement by tectonic plate movement, can and has occurred in the past, they contend, with relatively sudden slippage over thousands of miles of the earth's outer crust which has a depth of about thirty miles. Flem-Ath was a Canadian librarian who devoted his life to paleoarchaeology and wrote, with Wilson, that a 15 degree crustal shift occurred in the recent geological past, and that part of Antarctica was free of ice at that time. The last time this occurred, they say, was in 9600 BC. Prior to that time, about 50,000 years ago, the geography of the present-day North Pole had a different location in Hudson Bay, the Greenland Sea about 80,000 years ago, and about 100,000 BC there was still an earlier location in the Yukon. The location of famous historical cities in the world, they say, were often set up as markers of special interludes of latitude and longitude based on their orientation to pole locations at that time.

There are various theories that contend that Atlantis was not in the middle of the Atlantic Ocean. Ivar Zapp, professor at the University of Costa Rica and author of Atlantis in America, rejects the mid-Atlantic hypothesis because, he says, there is no evidence today of a continent-size civilization at the bottom of the ocean. He believes that Atlantis was actually all of North and South America; that Plato, when he spoke of the island of Atlantis, had in mind both of those continents and their connection at Central America. Yet, it requires a bit of a stretch of credulity to think that Plato, when speaking of the island of Atlantis, had in mind two vast continents. It is true that Plato was alluding to a huge continent size island mass. That is why it is difficult to accept the hypothesis put forward by some scholars that the small island of Santorini in the eastern Mediterranean was actually the site of Atlantis.

Zapp suggests that Poseidon, the capital of Atlantis, could have been in Costa Rica in the Diquis Delta in the southwest corner of Costa Rica which is protected from north winds by the mountains of central Costa Rica and, therefore, was able to maintain a warm climate in the years following the end of the Ice Age. He argues that after 10,000 BC the remnants of a civilization of a golden age struggled mightily to survive the cataclysm and to retain some part of the science and culture that had existed. Then, sometime between 8000 BC and 5000 BC, aided by the partial recollection of the science and technology of the first world civilization, new civilizations developed in the New World. They flourished until a few centuries before the Conquistadores arrived in Mexico. The Golden Age and the post-deluvian period up to the time of the Bronze Age, in his view, was one of international peace, advanced culture and a high level of technology, especially of astronomy and navigation by sea. Heyerdahl, through his excursions by boats built in the manner of the ancient peoples of Meso-America, proved to the world that ancient peoples could cross the Atlantic without much difficulty. But the academic world largely refused to accept that realization and continues to deny it today.

It was the survival of this ancient knowledge that allowed the magnificent Central American civilizations to grow, including the Olmecs, Toltecs, Incas, and Aztecs. By the time the Conquistadores came in 1519 the Aztec civilization was already in decline. Zapp argues that far from Europe having brought the blessing of civilization to the Americas, it was the other way around. He holds that Central America, as the center of world-wide sea navigation and trade, made possible an intermingling of world cultures that brought fresh ideas to Europe, the Near East, Egypt and Asia. He offers this as a new paradigm with which to interpret the archaeological mysteries of the world. In his paradigm, knowledge from Atlantis made possible the startling and early appearance of the Sphinx, the three Great Pyramids of Giza and the Ziggurats of Babylon. The facile movement of peoples by means of advanced navigational ability accounts for evidence of Caucasian, Black and Oriental peoples in the New World as indicated by sculptures and reliefs that have been discovered. The pyramids that were built in so many different areas of the world were done primarily for astronomical reasons: not to predict the seasons for planting which were known without such elaborate measures, but to aid navigation and perhaps to predict when another celestial catastrophe might occur. In answer to the question: Why is there so little evidence of ancient navigation, Zapp replies:

> There are several answers. The first is that advanced navigational cultures flourished before the deluge in seaports that are now buried hundreds of feet under the sea where little excavation has ever been done. The second answer is that boats and navigational instruments have been made from perishable goods. A third, and more important, answer is that there is evidence and quite a bit of it, but that no one operating within the traditional paradigm has been looking for it. (Zapp, p. 132)

A terrible coincidence in history—when the Aztecs were waiting hopefully for the white men to return, who they recalled as having brought them advanced knowledge earlier in mythological history—materialized in the form of 16th century Spaniards bringing death and destruction. Perhaps the Aztec reminiscence was of a time when various ethnic groups cohabited in the Americas. This could account for the evidence of a Phoenician presence in the Americas:

> Professor Barry Fell found ample evidence of Phoenician writing throughout the Americas. And with meticulous scholarship, Professor Cyrus Gordon confirmed the Paraiba Stone, found in Brazil in 1872, to be an authentic Phoenician inscription of the 6th century B.C. (Zapp, p. 65)

The Paraiba Stone has variously been described as a forgery and reaffirmed by some as authentic. But even if false, there have been other findings suggesting a Phoenician presence in the New World.

I accept as reasonable this new paradigm of an advanced Atlantean civilization, though its particulars, of course, await new information. The question of exactly where Atlantis was—that it was either under Antarctica, in the Atlantic Ocean, around Indonesia or in the New World—is not as critical as the concept that it did exist in some center or even in many centers, and that an international navigational sea expertise and an advanced technology allowed for communications between peoples of the world. This approach makes possible a new interpretation of ancient monuments throughout the world and, for our purposes, key monuments in Spain.

The dates for the earliest Central American phenomena may have preceded the Egyptian monuments. Zapp believes that some Mayan sites date back to 4000 BC—much earlier than is generally accepted by the dominant paradigm. The dominant paradigm offers the view that the construction of similar types of structures, like pyramidal temples in different parts of the world, was merely the result of equivalent levels of development, and that myths are of little value in understanding history and archaeology. Could it be, asks Zapp, that civilization and technology were primarily exported from the New World rather than the reverse and that behind the myths of Atlantis lies the key to a new understanding?

As in Egypt with the advent of the great pyramids of Giza, whose accepted origin is in the 3rd millenium BC, in Spain, the attribution of the supposedly great Islamic architectural achievements of the 8th to the 15th century AD offers no persuasive explanation as to how the advanced construction and artistic achievements were derived. I suggest that the Tartessians were people of Tartessos on the Iberian peninsula colonized by the Atlanteans; that their civilization was in many ways comparable or in advance of the Phoenicians, and that most of the alleged Islamic monuments were originally and basically of Phoenician construction but with much of their technique and style learned from the Tartessians. The relatively austere exteriors are reminiscent of ancient near eastern architecture; the glorious, colorful and innovative interiors perhaps derive mainly from Tartessos. Sorting out the cooperative relations between the two peoples remains to be done but there were apparently amicable and mutually supportive social and economic relations that must have resembled the type of close support found in the 10th century BC between the Phoenicians of Tyre under Hiram and the Jews in the regime of Solomon.

The Tartessians were originally peoples who had economic and cultural ties with Iberia or who had left their submerging Atlantic islands in order to find new lands in which to live. They were Atlanteans who may have sent out colonies along with their international trade. They may have introduced astronomical knowledge to England, making possible the first stages of the observatory at Stonehenge in the 3rd millenium BC. They may have provided the impetus for the Etruscan civilization. They may be the peoples who later became the Basques. And they may have been the people whose expertise made possible the creation of the temples of Malta in the 4th millenium BC.

It seems reasonable to assume that there may have been not one but two ancient disappeared advanced centers of civilization: Atlantis in the Atlantic Ocean and Lemuria in the Indian Ocean. The question of advanced technological achievements in ancient Egypt occurring in the third millennium with the relatively sudden achievement of the great Pyramids and, even prior to that, of the Sphinx is best accounted for, in my view, by the explanation that there was dissemination of advanced knowledge by people occupying a land area which was located, not in the Atlantic, but in the Indian Ocean. The Indus Valley Civilization in India, the Egyptian civilization and, perhaps, the Al Abaid pre-Sumerian civilization in Mesopotamia may owe their origins to Lemuria. To speculate as to whether the influence was from Atlantis or Lemuria may be of great interest but it is not the most important question. If there was an interconnected world culture in a Golden Age of advanced navigation and peaceful relations between countries whose origins preceded the end of the Ice Age, then influences on Egypt or Spain could have come from one or several interconnected sources.

The essential point is that the level of civilization found in pre-Pharaonic era in Egypt with its advanced achievements had to have originated from abroad. There have been theories advanced of aliens from other planets being the source of new developments. But there is no evidence for this, nor is it necessary to look beyond this planet for reasonable explanations. Yet, the ability of the Egyptians to handle extremely heavy stone pieces in their architecture represents a level of technology that seems to have no precedent in the region nor in any known region. Even larger stone pieces delivered to far less accessible terrain in the mountains occurred in Central America. And in Carnac in Brittany there are the fragmented remains of a 500 ton menhir. Attempts to duplicate the handling of gigantic stones in our times have not been successful even with our advanced technology. The Golden Age people must have known something about science and technology that made such movement reasonably efficient. That knowledge is now lost. Scientific knowledge has been lost in other periods and places. The European Dark Ages is illustrative of an historical era with retrogression in science.

We must consider the possibility that the oceans were no obstacle to early man prior to the Bronze Age. With his ships and his understanding of navigation he was able to communicate with and trade with peoples all over the globe. Those features of early civilization that we recognize as being remarkably similar at opposite ends of the earth are not the result of coincidence but result from communication between peoples. And we must recognize that the boundaries of land masses and their very existence did not necessarily evolve only by slow geological evolution but could have developed rapidly through cataclysmic events.

Alexander Kondratov, the Russian writer, in his <u>The Riddle of the Three Oceans</u> written in 1974, offers us many insights into a new geographical perspective that explains a different course of ancient human history. Instead of the slow, evolutionary changes in land masses, there were rapid shifts in the earth's crust, cataclysmic events that submerged existing land masses and brought new ones into existence. Movements occurred of the earth's crust with accompanying changes due to flood and earthquakes. From the contiguous landmass of Gawandaland, some 300 million years ago, break up and movement brought the continents into existence. There may have been other continents that existed before the end of the last Ice Age, 12,000-10,000 BC. It seems that there may have been three land masses of which only islands remain. One land mass extended from Indonesia out into the Pacific. Another, Atlantis, existed somewhere beyond the coast of Spain. And a third mass, Lemuria, was off the coat of Madagascar so that at one time Africa and Asia had a continuous land bridge. By the end of the last Ice Age only parts of Lemuria, islands like the Seychelles, remained in the Indian Ocean.

Advanced civilizations existed in all three areas long after they had broken up into smaller islands. From Lemuria came the Dravidian people who became the founders of the Indus Valley civilization and moved north to become the ancient Egyptians, the Al Abaid in Mesopotamia and the Elam civilization in Persia. From Atlantis came the Tartessians, the Etruscans, the Basques and, perhaps, some of the ancient peoples of Central and South America. From the Pacific land mass came the original inhabitants of Easter Island, the aborigines of Australia, pre-dynastic Egypt and the early civilizations of China.

From Africa or southeast Asia came the Olmecs of Mexico. The massive stone sculptures weighing up to 20 tons showing negroid features and other sculptures that have been discovered in Peru indicate that the predominant people among the Olmecs were negroid but that there were also Mayan and, perhaps, Phoenician peoples as well. The black peoples could not have been just slaves of the Phoenicians. The scale and monumental character of the statues plus their regal bearing indicate a ruling people. But we do not know from whence came the Canaanites, the original Phoenicians, or if they were indigenous to the Near East.

We know that the most active and enterprising of the maritime peoples in the Mediterranean from the 12th century to 6th century BC were the Phoenicians. They founded Cadiz as the Atlantic port of the Guadalquivir River in Andalusia in the 12th century BC, Europe's oldest city. They sailed from what is now roughly Lebanon to the opposite end of the Mediterranean and into the Atlantic in pursuit of gold, silver, copper and tin. It was the wealth of these cargoes that enabled them to pay tribute to the Assyrians and thereby stave off destruction from their powerful Near Eastern neighbor. But who was there in the Iberian peninsula for them to trade with? The Tartessians, whose origins we know little about, dwelt in Tartessos, the area mentioned in the Bible that Noah was returning from when he met calamity with the whale. Tartessos was probably centered in the Rio Tinto silver and copper mine area near Cadiz.

Of all the theories of Atlantis and its possible location, assuming it existed at all or perhaps it existed in only one main center, it seems most likely that Plato was correct in placing it in the Atlantic. It answers many questions to hypothesize that, prior to the rising of the sea levels after the last Ice Age in 10,000 BC there may have been a land mass in the mid-Atlantic with a civilization that continued to exist even as the land mass broke up into a network of islands whose enduring remains today are the Canary, Madeira, Azores and perhaps as far west as the islands of the Caribbean. This advanced maritime civilization, by 10,000 BC, had established colonies on the European continent which included Tartessos, the Basques in Spain, the Etruscans in Italy and perhaps even the first civilization in Egypt unless, as we have considered, Egypt's origin derives from Lemuria in the Indian Ocean.

The contradiction within Egyptian civilization that scholars have been unable to cope with is that it began at its most successful with apparently little prior development. The pyramids and the Sphinx were not the end product of a magnificent Egyptian civilization. These early products were basically without precedent. Recent attempts at dating the Sphinx have suggested an astonishing origin in the 8th millenium BC. The weathering of the stone suggests rain erosion rather than wind erosion according to Wilson and Flem-Ath in _The Atlantis Blueprint_ and supported by the geologist Robert M. Schoch in _The Voyage of the Pyramid Builders_. Thus, an extended period when North Africa had ample rain was the one in which the Sphinx was built rather than during the period of dessication that we know prevailed from the fourth millenium BC. This suggests that people from an enterprising maritime nation could have arrived from outside Egypt, perhaps hundreds or thousands of years earlier, to establish these magnificent structures or brought with them advanced technology for the indigenous people to use.

This would account for the leap in development of writing in Egypt. While we know there were autochthonous people in Egypt, they probably borrowed from exterior peoples the mode of writing with hieroglyphics that Egypt is so famous for. Kondratov points out that there is a missing link between the early pictograph writing of Egypt and the advanced hieroglyphics which was used at the time of the building of the pyramids that was the basis for their art and letters:

> It is easy to trace an inseparable connection between Egyptian hieroglyphics and Egyptian fine arts; they are based on a common style, a common attitude, a common model of the world. Hieroglyphic writing is part and parcel of Egyptian civilization. Why is it, asks Academician Tuayev, that by the time of the pyramids Egyptian writing was fully developed, and there was poetry, belles-lettres and scientific and legal literature, but there is no trace of how they all reached that level? There is no single answer to this question. (Kondratov, p.161)

And there is still no reasonable explanation for the handling of the 200 ton monolithic stones used in parts of the pyramid complex and the 1000 ton obelisks that the Egyptians are believed to have hewn, decorated and set up at that time. Even present day construction science can not handle the cutting and manipulation of these stone monoliths. If Egypt was not colonized from Atlantis, another possibility is that there existed another continent off the coast of India in the Indian Ocean referred to in ancient times as Lemuria. Or perhaps a landmass contiguous with the present day islands of Indonesia may have been the site of an advanced civilization. From these locations a maritime civilization could have extended its reach to create the first civilization of Egypt as well as the Al Ubaid civilization that preceded the Sumerians in Mesopotamia and its neighbor to the east of the Tigis-Euphrates-Elam.

The populations of Early Egypt, Al-Ubaid, Elam and the Dravidian peoples of south India as well as the indigenous peoples of Australia were all black. This suggests a common origin in Lemuria. This continent, like Atlantis, could have been a victim of rising seas, falling land and terrible earthquakes and floods. We know, since the acceptance of tectonic plate movement as a science in the 1960s, that the earth's surface is far more fluid than was ever imagined and that changes in land mass could come about much more quickly than expected. We know that the massive increase of the ocean waters after the last Ice Age in approximately the 12th to the 10th centuries BC produced rises of several hundred feet in the planet's ocean levels. Are there then drowned civilizations at the bottom of the Atlantic and Indian Oceans? Or perhaps even under the ice caps of Antarctica if we accept Hapgood's and Hancock's theories. Though not conclusive, there seems to be some archaeological evidence uncovered by oceanic archaeology that earlier civilizations did exist.

The center of the Atlantean cities in the Iberian peninsula was in the silver and copper region around Rio Tinto north of Cadiz called Tartessos. In order to be in close proximity to this rich resource and to have access to the Andalusian hinterland, the Phoenicians made use of the Guadalquivir River with Cadiz at its delta and developed Cordoba, a city as far up the river as their merchant boats could go. Cordoba was the political center of the Phoenician presence in Andalusia. To maintain military control they built, some three miles to the west of Cordoba, the military city which is now called Medina Azahara. To safeguard the Phoenician settlements along the south coast of Andalusia, they built a fortified citadel in the mountains close to the coast that came to be called the Alhambra. To trade with the Mediterranean and perhaps the New World, they set up several colonies on the Andalusian coast east of Gibraltar. They were mainly clustered in the vicinity of present-day Malaga and included: Cerro del Prado, Malaga, Toscanos, Morro de Mezquitilla, Chorreras and Almunecar.

To establish the religious, political and economic center of the Phoenician presence in Andalusia, they built within Cordoba, even before the city had developed, the administrative center, warehouse, temple and observatory known to us today as the Mosque of Cordoba. The complex was not built as an addition to an existing town; the town grew up around the complex. The building, as we shall see, had to satisfy commercial and astronomical requirements which narrowed its location to a specific site up the Guadalquivir River.

I have attempted to learn something about the construction history of the Mosque of Cordoba through Carbon-14 analysis. With the generous help of the Spanish government, I collected wood samples from the mosque and submitted five of them for analysis by two competent laboratories (Fig. Ia). The results, with 90% probability, were as follows:

> Sample #1: In 1983, a sample of roof beam that was stored in the mosque produced a date range of 1195-1520 AD. The mid-point date is 1325 AD, plus or minus 65 years.
> Sample #2: In 1983, a piece of roof beam taken from the roof of the Stage IV area produced a date range from 1030 BC to 580 BC. The mid-point date is 810 BC, plus or minus 80 years.
> Sample #3: In 1990, a wood beam sample taken in situ in the Stage IV area of the roof resulted in a date range of 420 AD to 670AD with a mid-point date of 600 AD, plus or minus 70 years.
> Sample #4: In 1990, a sample of wood panel from the ceiling of the mosque which was stored nearby in the Palacio Episcopal, had a date range of 670 AD to 941 AD. The mid-point date is 785 AD, plus or minus 50 years.
> Sample #5: In 1990, a sample of a wood beam embedded in the interior masonry wall of the minaret produced a date range of 640 AD to 880 AD. The mid-point date is 681 AD, plus or minus 60 years.
> Two American laboratories were used to Carbon-14 date the five samples. Sample #1 was prepared by Dr. William Evans, then Professor of Chemistry at Brooklyn College in New York, later to become Dean of the School of Science, in his Carbon-14 laboratory. The lab is currently discontinued. Samples #2-5 were analyzed by the Beta Analytic labs at Coral Gables, Florida, which was headed by Dr. Murray A. Tamers. (Mills, "The Pre-Islamic Provenance of the Mosque of Cordoba", 1991)

Of special significance is sample #2 which produced a reading of 810 BC! If this sample is valid, not contaminated, nor a freak anomaly, then it falls within the Phoenician era. Note the in situ exposed roof beam and its hole which I drilled to obtain the wood sample for Carbon-14 dating (Pl. Ia). The wood was so hard from centuries of petrification that it took three core drills to extricate the 2 inch by ½ inch diameter sample. I used one of the first hand-held cordless drills, produced by Makita, since there was no electric power in that location. The scattering of the other carbon-14 dates would seem to indicate that the mosque had a long and varied history of rebuilding and being added to, perhaps because of fires and earthquakesas well as demographic needs. In any case, the role of scientific dating is unquestionably of paramount value in future research on the mosque. These samples suggest an earlier origin of the mosque. Could it have been built by the Romans?

Pl. Ia
Carbon-14 sample source
from hole in roof beam

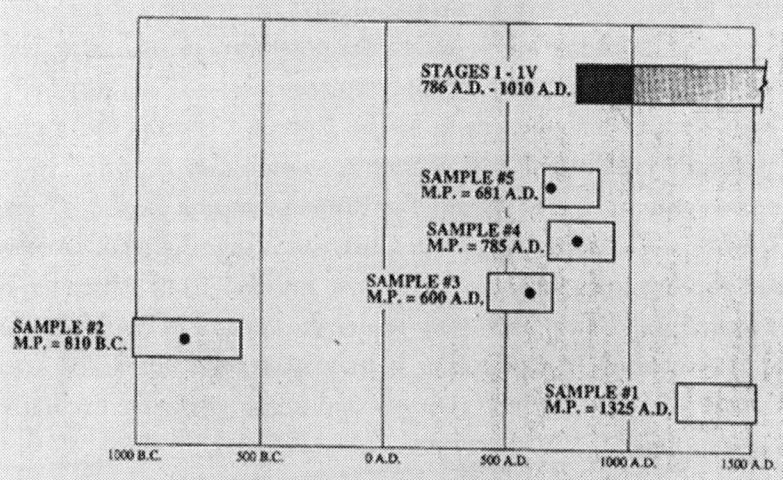

Fig. Ia
Mid-Points of Carbon-14 Analysis

2

Roman Antecedents

An earlier investigation that I pursued to solve the mystery of the origin of the Mosque of Cordoba was to weigh the possibility of its having been originally a Roman warehouse, perhaps from around the 1st century AD, a time of high Roman achievement in Spain. Roman Cordoba was a great Roman political, intellectual and economic center that exported much needed metals and grain throughout the Roman Empire. In the 5th century AD, Roman Cordoba fell to the Christian Visigoths who, in turn, succumbed to Muslim conquerors who first invaded from Africa in 711 AD. As a reused warehouse previously under the control of the Visigoths, it seemed reasonable to imagine that it may have been converted later, with relatively minor structural changes and some cosmetic decorative changes, to a mosque.

Southern Spain had a long and exciting history shared by Celt-Iberians, Tartessians, Phoenicians, Carthaginians, Jews, Romans, Visigoths, Arabs and Berbers prior to the Reconquista by the Christians from the north of Spain in the 12th century AD. What later came to be known as the Mosque of Cordoba, the Alhambra and Medina Azahara were awesome buildings and complexes that were added to, replaced, destroyed and modified over the centuries. What preceded their Muslim incarnation and how much of the past was incorporated in their structures is a matter of controversy. Yet, the twelfth centennial of the Mosque of Cordoba which took place in 1986 commemorated its de novo construction in 786 AD. I challenge the concept of the origin of all three monuments as being Islamic. Medina Azahara is said to have been built de novo in the 10th century AD. The Alhambra was supposedly built by Nasrid Muslims in the 14th and 15th centuries AD by making use of the foundations on the site of a previously existing fort. All three real origins and development, I maintain, are quite different.

It is not the paucity of hard historical data alone that prompted me to raise questions regarding the origin of the Mosque of Cordoba. Certain architectural and decorative features of the mosque cannot be explained adequately within the context of what is accepted concerning the early development of Islamic art and architecture. And, apparently, no precedent existed in Islamic Spain for a mosque of that scale. It is doubtful that the Arab and Berber invaders, who were nomadic peoples in their homelands of Arabia, Syria and the Maghreb and, therefore, not accustomed to massive urban construction, were capable of producing anything in Spain on the technical or artistic level of that splendid mosque. Furthermore, there is no evidence of a crescendo of development leading up to its construction. Nor was there any spread of non-dynastic works following its completion. There is also confusion about the duration of construction.

The mosque's location on the periphery of the city in a prime commercial area is unusual. Congregational, Friday mosques, are generally integral with the fabric of the city and accessible to as many people as possible; thus, mosques usually have the advantage of a central location. This building's location on the Guadalquivir River, next to a Roman bridge, adjacent to the Roman quay and docks, and accessible to the fine Roman roads extending in four directions would support the Roman warehouse hypothesis, whereas its location would not be supportive of the centrality to the city's population that would be expected were it a mosque. Why did the Romans build this bridge precisely in conjunction with the mosque when the mosque had, we are told, not been built yet? From an engineering point of view this location may have been most convenient. Or it may be that a very important structure was already in place which was an invitation for a bridge infrastructure that could help service it.

The building's elongated first three stages fits neatly into the needs of a Roman warehouse. The warehouse would have allowed goods to be stored close to what seems to have been the adjacent road to the east, located under what was later assumed to be Stage IV. The Stage III mihrab may have been used as a Roman shrine or altar, not unusual in a Roman warehouse. The court was suitable for a staging area for products that, if necessary, could have been kept under cover in the surrounding porticoes.

According to scholars who have studied the mosque, it underwent four stages of development from 786 AD to 1002 AD. All the stages are said to be Islamic. It is my contention that the first three stages and the existing surrounding wall were pre-Islamic. I had initially thought they might be Roman. According to the accepted paradigm, Stage I had eleven naves or longitudinal aisles and eight cross-aisles built by Abd ar-Rahman I. Stage II consisted of 11 more cross-aisles added by Abd ar-Rahman II from 822 AD to 951 AD and included a 23.75 meter expansion of the court to the north during the reign of Abd ar-Rahman III in 951 AD. However, there is no mention in any contemporary documents of any construction nor of any additional stages to construction. The earliest references appear some two hundred years later. Al Hakam II is said to have built fourteen more cross-aisles in stage III. Al-Mansur, in his Stage IV, we are told, added eight longitudinal aisles on the east side of the mosque, thereby increasing the total longitudinal aisles from eleven to nineteen. The alleged reasoning behind this was to accommodate the increased number of believers, to make the mosque into a more normal and less elongated shape, and to avoid the problem of the proximity of the river which discouraged building an extension in that direction and the need to again demolish and rebuild the mihrab if the extension had been further south.

However, as a Roman warehouse, goods could have been stored close to a probable road to the east, located under what was later assumed to be Stage IV. As a warehouse it is comparable to the famous Porticus Aemilia built outside Rome in the second century BC. The elongated, oblong shape of the warehouse compares in form to the alleged Stage III form of the Mosque of Cordoba. According to William MacDonald, the noted historian on ancient Rome, the Porticus Aemilia was:

> a vast warehouse on the east bank of the Tiber ... composed of some 200 barrel-vaulted chambers in long tiered rows, it covered an area 60 x 487 meters. The vaults did not rest upon solid walls, but rather upon perforated supports resembling pier arcades so that each chamber was open laterally as well as axially to its neighbors. The result was a practi-

cal, fire-resistant building of ordered clarity, well-suited to warehousing and trans-shipping goods. (MacDonald, <u>The Architecture of the Roman Empire, An Introductory Study</u>, pp. 5-6)

The Mosque of Cordoba's hypostyle hall of columns, its two-way circulation, and its vast enclosed space would have served well as a warehouse for, first, the Phoenicians and later the Romans.

The inconsistency of the end aisles being narrower than all the other aisles of the first three stages raises further questions as to its origin as a mosque which normally has uniformly wide aisles except perhaps for the center aisle. As a warehouse, however, it may have responded to special administrative needs along the interior perimeter. What have been assumed to be discontinuities in construction between the stages may be no more than separations designed for fire protection or as areas designated to store different materials.

Another interesting feature that could support the argument for a Roman origin is evidence that, unlike a typical mosque, it may not have been built on one level. Excavations under the mosque reveal rooms and probably a street some four to five meters below the floor level, down to the level of Roman Cordoba (Mackendrick, <u>Romans on the Rhine</u>, p. 221). The rooms are paved with mosaics that appear to be Roman. A room which I reached by a ladder through a removable piece of stone flagging in Stage I was paved with orange, dark red, black and white tesserae laid in geometric patterns; in one section was depicted an amphora. The mosaic pavement continued under the wall on one side, suggesting that the surrounding brick partition wall may have been a later construction. The room apparently coincided with a single structural bay above and its ceiling was about three meters high. Further investigation should determine how the floor of the mosque is structurally supported above these bays or rooms.

Whereas a mosque would not have been built on two levels, a warehouse might have been so constructed. If grain was stored on the upper level it would have benefited from the drying effect of the air circulating beneath the floor. The Roman double warehouse at Trier in Germany consisted of a pair of two-storied warehouses, each about 70.1 meters long and 19.8 meters wide built in the early 4th century AD. The loading yard passed between the two buildings. The floor of the upper story was carried on two longitudinal rows of stone piers:

> The traveler from Gaul, reaching the city by the [Roman] bridge would have an impressive view of the ornate east gate, the massive baths beside it, and the double-warehouse, symbol of prosperity … (Mackendrick, <u>Romans on the Rhine</u>, p. 221)

It is possible that the same relationship that existed at Trier of bridge, archway and warehouse may have prevailed at Cordoba.

Roman warehouses were fortified to provide security for the valuable goods stored within. The popular Roman building method of using alternating headers and stretchers to add strength to the wall is also used in the exterior walls of the Mosque of Cordoba. This feature, along with its crenellated roof and heavy buttressing piers, give the mosque the general appearance of being fortified. The building's buttresses are probably not needed to support the well-built exterior walls and wood roof framing; rather, they may have been intended to withstand the lateral thrust of stored merchandise, such as grain, that would have been piled up loose against the exterior walls on the upper level. The marble grilles in the walls would have provided proper ventilation; the lower level would have been suitable for heavy metals. Scholars have argued that the Muslims who built the mosque imitated Roman masonry techniques, possibly using as a model the nearby Roman bridge. What seemed more reasonable to me early in the investigation was that both the mosque and the bridge were Roman and built at the same time, during the Augustan era, the 1st century BC to the 1st century AD.

It has been argued that the multiple arch construction often employed in Roman bridge and aqueduct construction such as the aqueduct at Merida was clearly an inspiration for the double arches employed in the prayer hall in the Mosque of Cordoba. There is a resemblance but Roman construction does not include horseshoe arches as in the mosque. However, this similarity did initially contribute to my earlier consideration that the mosque may have been built by the Romans.

A second underground area was inspected below Stage IV adjacent to stage I (Pl. XIIa). It was larger than the other room, comprising several bays running north and south along what appeared to be a former roadway. If this was a roadway it was probably on the level of Roman Cordoba. A set of masonry steps connects the roadway with the mosque level. Clearly, a detailed study of both areas and adjacent ones would reveal the full extent of the lower level construction. The columns or piers that exist below are point supports that transmit the loads from the upper level with the same layout of bays below as above. The infill walls are probably non load-bearing and of post-Roman construction. It may be that the lower level is coextensive with parts or all of the four building stages.

Cordoba as a city was probably in use by the Phoenicians although I can offer no direct evidence for this assertion. But it is known that the Phoenicians had many active trading posts and settlements in Andalusia. Could Cordoba have been one of them? It is said to have been founded by the Carthaginians who struggled with the Romans for control of Spain but were finally defeated by the Romans in 214 BC. Cordoba became a Roman settlement with a stockade enclosure with the establishment by Marcio of a Roman encampment in 206 BC to the north of the Carthaginian city. It was further developed by Marcelo in 169 BC who encircled it with a stone wall. In 29 BC. Augustus extended Roman Cordoba south to the Guadalquivir River and it became the capital of Baetica, known by the Muslims as Andalusia. From Baetica came the Roman emperors Trajan and Hadrian. From Cordoba came Seneca the rhetorician; his son, a famous Stoic philosopher; and the latter's nephew, Lewcanus the poet—all born around the 1st century AD.

Cordoba was a great Roman cultural, intellectual and economic center. Cordoba and other cities supplied Rome with precious metals and grain which made it worthwhile for Rome to spend great sums of money and manpower to subdue the Celt-Iberians, the indigenous people. These indigenous peoples undoubtedly had absorbed the earlier Tartessian and Phoenician peoples. Following the Visigothic interlude in the 6th and 7th centuries, the Muslim conquerors invaded in 7II AD and established Cordoba as their capital in 765 AD. Abd ar-Rahman I is credited with building Stage I of the mosque in 786 AD. It is reputed to have been the first mosque of any consequence in Cordoba.

It is important to note that no extant documents of the 8th century AD allude to the mosque's construction or rehabilitation. It was not until two hundred years later, in the 10th century, that al-Razi relates how Abd al-Rahman I dismantled the church of St. Vincent located on the bank of the Guadalquivir River to clear a site for the building of the Great Mosque. According to al-Razi, the church had replaced an earlier Roman temple. This belief has been challenged by some leading scholars. K.A.C. Creswell, the great scholar who wrote four huge volumes on early Muslim architecture in 1932, argues that the story was devised to parallel the legend of the origin of the Mosque of Damascus in Syria built, it is said, in 715 AD:

> Ibn Adhari and al-Maqqari say that after the conquest the Muslims acted on the precedent set by Khalid ibn al-Walid after the capture of Damascus, and took half of the largest church in Cordova and used it as a mosque. Terrasse has pointed out that this story so closely resembles that of the Great Mosque of Damascus, that one is led to ask if it has not been invented afterwards by the chroniclers. I believe the truth of the matter to be that Ibn Jubayr brought the Damascus legend to Spain at the end of the twelfth century, that it became linked with the Cordova mosque shortly afterwards, then incorporated in the spurious chronicle of ar-Razi in circulation in the thirteenth century, and adopted by Ibn Adhari and al-Maqqari. (Creswell, A Short Account of Early Muslim Architecture, p. 213)

Al-Razi called the Mosque of Damascus the inspiration for the Mosque of Cordoba. Henri Terrasse, the French scholar and writer, citing research by Felix Hernandez, states that the Church of St.Vincent must have been demolished since, he admits, no reliable evidence exists of its foundations:

> Les fouilles faites récemment dans la grande mosquée par D. Félix Hernandez prouvent definitement que l'église Saint-Vincent fut entièrement démolie. On ne peut retrouver ses fondations. (Terrasse, L'Art Hispano-Mauresque des Origines au XIIe Siècle, p. 59) *(The research made recently on the great mosque by D. Flix Hernandez definitely proves*

that the church of St. Vincent was entirely demolished. Its foundations cannot be found).

There is a curious parallel sequence of events that led to both the accepted belief of the construction of the Mosque of Damascus and the Mosque of Cordoba. In both cases an existing Christian cathedral was taken over, compensated for, then demolished to make way for a grand mosque. But Terrasse finds it all slightly incredible:

> L'histoire de la fondation de la grande mosquée de Cordoue rapelle tellement celle de la grande mosquée de Damas qu'on est amène´ a se demander si ce parallelisme presque rigoureux des deux fondations omeiyades n'a pas eté imaginé après coup par les chroniquers. (Terrasse, p. 59) *(The history of the foundation of the great mosque of Cordoba recalls so closely that of the grand mosque of Damascus that one is led to question whether that almost exact parallelism of the two Ummayad constructions has not been imagined after the fact by the chroniclers.)*

Manuel Gomez-Moreno also finds no evidence of any previous church:

> Intrega averiguar cómo sería aquella iglesia mayor de San Vicente, predecesora suya. Se has explorado, has poco años, el subsuelo para rebajar el pavimento, sin descrubir nada que pudiera corresponderle. A gran profundidad aparecieron mosaicos romanos y cimientos de casas; encima, a unos 55 centimetros del piso moderno, la cepa de un edificio ruin, con solería de hormigon y paredes de mampostería mala, formando tres naves dirigidas de oriente a poniente, cuyo ancho total no pasaba de 12 metros; y, ya en el patio, a dos de profundidad, la ruina de otro edificio romano tardio: gran pórtico rematado en exedras, habitaciones a su parte oriental y delante cinco columnas, con capitales de tipo corintio degenerado, provistos de dos filas de hojas lisas simplemente, fustes de pudinga mal redondeados y basas áticas: ni su situacion ni su aspecto corresonden a lo que se buscaba. (Gomez-Moreno, <u>Ars Hispaniae</u>, Vol. III, pp. 19-20) *(It is intriguing to investigate how its predecessor, the main church of San Vicente, could have been. The basement has been studied for a few years, in order to expose the floor level, without discovering anything that could correspond to it. At considerable depth appeared Roman mosaics and foundations of houses; above which, at*

about 55 centimeters of modern flooring, the remains of a ruined edifice, with concrete base and walls of poor masonry, consisting of three naves oriented east to west, whose total width did not exceed 12 meters; and, similarly in the patio. At two meters depth, the ruins of another late Roman building: a great portico fitted out with exedras, dwellings in the eastern part and in front of which were five columns, with capitals of a corrupted Corinthian style, provided simply with two rows of leaves, shafts of poorly rounded flutings and Attic bases: neither its placement nor appearance corresponded to what was sought.)

The lack of evidence could also suggest that the Church of St. Vincent was never built. The accepted view that the ancient Roman church was cleared away and a grand new mosque built on the site appears to be even less credible in that during the early Umayyad years in Spain, 756-788, Cordoba witnessed a period of continuous bloody uprisings and murderous intrigues, reducing the likelihood of massive financial allocations for an elaborate mosque at that time. In those historical periods lacking in substantial evidence one must rely on maximum plausibility when seeking unavoidably tentative explanations for events. At this point, it is more reasonable to assume the prior existence of the three monuments—the Mosque of Cordoba, the Alhambra and Medina Azahara—then their having been built by the Muslims.

As for the theory of the mosque's Roman origin, I would now, on stylistic grounds, rule it out. The Romans did not make use of indigenous styles; they cast everything in the Roman mold. The interlaced and arabesque arches would have been anathema to them. I believe now that the commonality of Mediterranean construction during the Roman era and prior to it accounts for what we interpret now as Roman features. The Romans were engineers but not as creative esthetically in the way that we understand the Greeks or the Minoans, and in my judgment, the Phoenicians, to have been creative. The bridge across the Guadalquivir was theirs but not the mosque. Those delightful arabesques and marvelous interlaced cupolas could not have been theirs. The forest of columns layout could be interpreted as common to warehouses and administrative centers serving various communities and states within the early Mediterranean.

3

Scholarship Takes a Holiday

The somewhat apocryphal story of how the Umayyad dynasty was founded in Spain is so bizarre that it has much in common with a Hollywood spectacle. The rival clan in Damascus, the Abassids, devised a plan to eliminate their rivals, the ruling Umayyads. They invited all the Umayyad royalty to a peace dinner at the palace in Baghdad to reconcile their differences. Once there, all the Umayyads were slaughtered except Abd ar-Rahman and his cousin who ran for their lives towards Africa. At a river the Abassids caught up with them. Abd ar-Rahman swam to safety on the opposite shore. His cousin fell behind and was murdered. Abd ar-Rahman's flight eventually took him all the way across north Africa to Morocco where, with the aid of friendly supporters, he was able to cross over to Spain and to establish himself with the existing Umayyad forces which had arrived years earlier in 711 AD and gained their hold on southern Spain. He proceeded to consolidate his position and become the political leader of the Umayyad regime in Spain. In Damascus, the Abassids set up a new dynasty, moved their headquarters to Baghdad, and ruled until the city's destruction by the Mongols in 1248 AD.

The Muslims, led by Abd ar-Rahman I, established an independent kingdom in Spain in 756 AD and proclaimed Cordoba their capitol. It is said that he founded and built the First Stage of the Mosque of Cordoba in 786 AD. This great achievement was said to have been made as a marvelous leap of creativity, perhaps due to some innate Muslim ability. The scholarly consensus on the historical contribution to art and architecture in their original homelands by these early Muslims—Syrians, Beduins and Berbers—was minimal. While their development of the Arabic language through their poetry and calligraphy had reached esthetic heights, their development of architecture was limited to not much more than tents and adobe huts. The Berbers were the most numerous. They were attracted from Africa by the prospect of fruits of pillage and war. In the period of their first penetration of Iberia from 711 AD to 750 AD the Muslims, Terrasse tells us, built next to nothing, the Africans least of all:

> Ni ces soldats orientaux, ni ces primitifs quiétaient les Berbères ne pouvaient alors rien créer, surtout dans le domaine de l'art. (Terrasse, p. 52) *(Neither the eastern soldiers, nor those primitives who were the Berbers could create anything, especially in the domain of art.)*

Apparently, existing buildings were made use of, rather than new ones built. The turmoil within Andalusia left little time or potential to engage in magnificent new works. From 711 to 750 AD a succession of governors routinely assassinated each other. In 755 AD Abd ar-Rahman I at the age of 25 landed at Almuneçar on the southern coast of Andalusia. After thirty years of continuous warfare we are told that he turned his hand to building the First Stage of the Mosque of Cordoba from 785 AD to 786 AD. The first part of the Second Stage was allegedly built by Abd ar-Rahman II from 822 AD to 852 AD, then added to by Abd ar-Rahman III from 912 AD to 961 AD. The Third Stage is attributed to Hakam II from 961 AD to 976 AD. Stage Four is said to have been built in 987 AD by Al Mansur, the prime minister and real power in the reign of Hisham II. None of the above is actually proven. Probably, work was done to repair the destruction and disrepair that had occurred over centuries. But there is no real evidence for this accepted scenario of successive stages of new construction.

However, by the tenth century the Umayyads had achieved a high level of stability and prosperity. Having broken away from the influence of the caliphate in Baghdad by proclaiming a new caliphate in Spain, and by sharing a degree of "convivencia", a living together in relative harmony, with Jews and Christians, they were able to attain a Golden Age of culture. Art, poetry and architecture flourished. Immense libraries were at hand for scholars. While Europe was still in the thrall of its Dark Ages, Spain was leading the way to a brighter future. But not all great works of architecture that have been attributed to them as being built de novo were in fact their original creations. Nonetheless, their ability to make use of the existing structures, to enhance them or modify them for their own purposes, made it possible to preserve them for centuries to come, even to the present. Historical accuracy is, of course, critical in order to establish the real sources of Spanish cultural achievements, including negative developments. The propensity for Muslim armies to conquer foreign lands and to make use of existing structures to establish their new regimes, to refashion these buildings to suit their cultural needs and then to present them as having been their own new accomplishments, is a syndrome in many areas of the Muslim world that has yet to be researched adequately by scholars. From Spain to India and the lands in between, wherever Muslim hegemony has prevailed, the true authorship of ancient buildings must be reexamined. This is especially true where the lands that were usurped had affluent cultures with numerous cities and buildings which may have been spared destruction and used by their new masters, perhaps with different functions.

Scholarship on medieval Spain informs us that the three most famous Islamic monuments in Spain are the Mosque of Cordoba, the palatial city of Azahara, and the fortress city of the Alhambra. We must examine the evidence for their alleged Islamic origins and test the arguments that have traditionally been espoused to support this thesis. It is the contention of this writer that these three monuments that are claimed to have originated in the Islamic period of Spain, from the 8th through the 15th centuries AD, were originally built in a previous era, the Phoenician era from the 12th to the 7th century BC, considerably prior to the 800 years of Islamic occupation. What we know of these three magnificent complexes has been derived mainly from second-hand evidence of later historians and court chroniclers. Hard evidence is lacking.

The origin of the Mosque of Cordoba, for example, is known to us primarily by writings composed some 200 hundred years after the building was said to have been built. Writings on the subject appeared of which the works of Isa ibn Ahmad al-Razi are the most important. However, we know of his writings only from quotations appearing in works by later writers, principally al Makkari in the seventeenth century. The observations of al-Razi may have actually described an existing older building rather than one built in Islamic times. Islamic references to the building could have referred mistakenly to a building that was refurbished rather than one built de novo. Nor can we count on the common sense approach which leads us to reason that because it looks Islamic then the only outstanding question is: how did Islam come to build it? Its looks could be the result of later identification by standards that have been applied for centuries to what we consider to be essentially Islamic forms and designs.

How did the Umayyad dynasty of Spain, in the early years of Islam in the 8th, 9th and 10th centuries, find the time, ability and impetus to build so masterfully? Admittedly, the authoritarian character of their regimes was not necessarily an insuperable obstacle to great and sensitive architecture. We know that Louis XIV was ruthless yet still capable of building Versailles. But in the Iberian Islamic interlude prior to the tenth century, the main thrust of the occupation was its goal of exploiting and looting of the magnificent existing treasures of Spain rather than building a great civilization. The reign of Abd ar-Rahman I (756-788) was filled with endless war and insurrection. He was widely detested. Instability continued during the reign of his son Hisham I (786-796) who allegedly built the first minaret of the Mosque of Cordoba in 793 AD thereby completing, what I call for convenience, Stage I of construction. Hakam I (796-822) is said to have continued the construction even though the excesses of his regime brought the people to open rebellion. There ensued a century of lawlessness until Abd ar-Rahman III (912-961), in a period of prosperity, is said to have demolished the existing minaret, enlarged the mosque to the north, and built the second minaret. Any witnesses to early Muslim construction or rehabilitation have remained silent. Those that followed, being Muslims and in the service of the regimes, had an incentive to continue the deception. The various epigraphic Koranic statements on the buildings could have been inserted afterwards to bolster the illusion.

Clouding our understanding of the actual earlier origin is the prevalence of a bias against the Phoenicians that permeated 19th century historiography. This was largely due to the influence of anti-Semitism which established an unfortunate precedent for later scholarship up to the present. Because the Phoenicians were Semites they were identified with the Jews of Europe. Martin Bernal, classics scholar at Cornell, has made an excellent case for the influence of anti-Semitism on scholarship regarding the Phoenicians in his books <u>Black Athena</u>, Vols. I and II and <u>Black Athena Writes Back</u>. Scholars, perhaps without realizing their bias, tended to ignore the role of the Phoenicians in history. It was not until after World War II, when anti-Semitism had largely become discredited, that a certain amount of objectivity was possible. At the same time, the romantic attitudes then developing toward the East tended to encourage the acceptance of an idealized Islamic sensitivity to beauty. Yet, to this day, the amount of money, time and interest in Phoenician archaeology and culture is overshadowed by the preponderance of interest in ancient Greece, Rome and even Carthage. The many Phoenician sites in and around the Mediterranean remain to be excavated to a far greater extent than they have been.

An outstanding scholar of the 19th century was the archaeologist Ernest Renan who shared the negative bias against the Phoenicians with his contemporaries. The prevalent view, that survives even to this day, was that the Phoenicians were crass commercial traders who could borrow from their more culturally sensitive neighbors like the Egyptians and the Greeks but could not create art at a commensurate level They produced many art objects that reflected the influence of their neighbors. They could build and they could navigate but artistically they were said to be second-rate. As a case in point, Renan in discussing the architecture of the Phoenicians speaks contemptuously of their style:

> Even the capitals of the columns at Um-el-Awamid are not alike; in the portions which most evidently correspond the details are different. (Renan, <u>Mission de Phénicie</u>, p. 822)

A design standard that he considers absolute—the uniformity of columns—need not be applied in all countries and at all times. The columns in the Mosque of Cordoba vary considerably. Scholars attribute this to the reuse of older Roman or Visigothic columns in the construction of the mosque. But it could be argued that these were Phoenician columns being used in the traditional Phoenician style, which as Renan admits is typical of their practice.

Perhaps the chief obstacle to reevaluating the origins of the three Spanish monuments in question is psychological. When confronted with what might seem to the average reader to be an absurd contention—that the monuments are actually much older than the experts have claimed, that in fact they were older buildings that were rehabilitated by Islam—the reader has usually reacted by saying: "But they look Islamic!" However, it is widely acknowledged that the style that has come to be known as "Islamic" is identified by features that Islam, for the most part, either found or borrowed. There was no inhibition on the part of the Islamic conquerors to occupy buildings, sacred or secular, and reuse them for their own purposes. This is in marked contrast to Hindu tradition which forbids the reuse of another religion's structure as a Hindu temple. This helps explain why many Hindu palaces in India were appropriated to become tombs and mosques which the Muslims knew could then never be reclaimed by the infidel Hindus who regarded the buildings as contaminated.

Islam began in the deserts of Arabia, among a people with little prior expertise of architecture other than the setting up of their own tents. Though there were many ancient ruins in Arabia, any Arab interest in them was limited by their poverty and by their antipathy to pre-Islamic knowledge. They were a nomadic people who lived under harsh conditions. It was through their conquests of affluent states that they were brought into contact with the advanced architecture of civilizations with which, as conquerors, they had to accommodate. They adapted to what they found by either destroying or converting the buildings to their new functions, depending on their needs in each region.

In the most affluent areas that they conquered they found no need to build anew. There was a bountiful built environment full of structures for them to choose from. This was especially true of India, Spain and Persia. That is why many of the greatest so-called Islamic buildings of these countries are not actually originally Islamic. The greatest contribution of Islam to world architecture is not that they built buildings like the Taj Mahal but that they spared them from oblivion by using them for their new urban and imperial needs. In other countries, like those in North Africa, Turkey and Central Asia, there may have been a greater need for new construction. In Central Asia, it is well known that Islam spared the lives of captured artisans and architects. In the late 14th and early 15th centuries, Tamerlane would save craftsmen from the terror of annihilation and distribute them throughout the empire to use their expertise. In some cases, as in India, the Muslims knew of the reluctance of the indigenous Hindu peoples to reoccupy a former temple that had been converted to a mosque and, therefore, been "defiled". They used the conversions as a form of political domination.

Having complete control of the media, the occupying Islamic regimes asserted that they had built the edifices and gardens. Who could contest them? Even visitors were guided to see what it was deemed important for them to see. The result has been a massive disinformation campaign extending over many centuries and countries. These assertions have now congealed into a rote repetition of what passes for history. What was original with the Muslims, as compared to what they found and reused, has to be sorted out by contemporary scholars based on realistic appraisals and not on the weight of past opinion. The high standards of evidence that are generally applied in the physical sciences must be employed, as far as possible, in Islamic studies to correct the accumulated distortion of our body of knowledge.

4
Unity of Style

Not only do the construction details suggest a common origin in time of the so-called first three stages and the entire surrounding wall, but one must consider the implications as to the origin of the mosque of the apparent unity of composition and style throughout. L. Torres Balbas is struck by this phenomena:

> Los siglos han hecho *el milagro* (my italics) de fundir obras tan lejanas en su aspecto formal y en su cronología, como son la fachada de la mezquita al patio y la torre. Con la vegetación y la fuente barroca forman un conjuncto perfecto, acabado, de completa armonía." (Torres Balbas, <u>La Mezquita de Cordoba y las Ruinas de Madinat al-Zahra</u>, p. 94) *(The centuries have brought about the miracle of fusing works so disparate in their formal aspect and chronology, such as the façade of the mosque and the patio and tower. They end up by forming a complete harmony including the vegetation and the fountain).*

The building's first three stages show a seamless continuity of construction and style. He considers it a "miracle" that for over 200 years this unity was maintained. There is in reality a simple explanation: Its first three stages were, in fact, built at the same time. Stage IV, not including its exterior wall, must have been built later, having discontinuities that we will examine.

Of course, there would normally be a strong tendency for a building constructed even over a 200 year period, with additions being continually made, to follow the same theme. Each successive addition may well have had its design motivated by an architect anxious to carry out the original theme. But, at the same time, due to breaks of long intervals, sometimes many decades, one would also expect discontinuities of style. But we find that the battlements, the arches, the wall/pier relationship, the detailing, all seem to be designed at once. This would demonstrate a remarkable display of discipline on the part of the many architects involved for two centuries in staying true to the original character—unless it was in fact built at the same time.

The standard explanation offered by scholars for this remarkable situation is put forth by Nuha N. N. Khoury, an associate professor in the Department of Art and Architecture at the University of California in Santa Barbara who specializes in Islamic architecture. She believes that there is an organic continuity between the first significant Muslim building, the Prophet's mosque in Medina, and the Mosque of Cordoba. She claims that in wishing to establish the legitimacy of the Cordoba caliphate in the tenth century, Al-Hakam fashioned his expansion to the south—Stage III—to reflect the original power of the Umayyads. Thus, he not only avoided correcting the non-Mecca alignment of Abd Ar-Rahman I's Stage I but purposefully continued the style of the earlier phase, though enhancing it with more elaborate developments in the maqsura, in order to glorify the reestablishment of the Umayyad caliphate in Cordoba.

The identification of the Mosque of Cordoba with the history of Islam is further strengthened by the happy coincidence of there being a church on the site of the Mosque of Damascus in the 7th century—the church of Saint John—which was previously demolished just as the church of St. Vincent was claimed to have been demolished in Cordoba to make way for the new mosque. The assertion by Khoury, that we are dealing with myth-making, does not shake her belief that the Mosque of Cordoba was in origin Islamic:

> Tenth and post-tenth century histories of the Cordoba mosque express the symbolic appropriation of the history of Islam in al-Andalus by constructing *a mythical identity* (my italics) for the monument that parallels that of earlier Umayyad architectural artifacts. The intent of the myth of the church of St. Vincent is most clearly revealed through its predecessor, that of the church of Saint John of Damascus, and through the image of the Umayyads as upholders of Islam that is

implied by this myth. (Khoury, *"The meaning of the Great Mosque of Cordoba in the tenth century"*, p. 84)

It seems not to have occurred to Khoury that if the Cordoba story is a later writing of myth, then perhaps the earlier Damascus history was also a myth.

If we examine the parapet on top of the wall that encloses the building we will note some changes in style but, by and large, a continuity is maintained throughout. In any case, where there is a change in the ashlar stone pieces they do not correspond to what should have been discontinuities in stages of construction. Thus, where one would normally expect to find a construction joint between supposed phases of construction, they do not exist And, in general, the relation between parapet style and supposed stages do not correspond.

Faithfulness to style in the four stages of construction is demonstrated in the use of the horseshoe arch, the red and white alternating voussoirs of the arches, the gabled roof formations, the mode of the hypostyle hall, the paneled ceiling, the use of random columns, stone grilles on the exterior walls, etc. Therefore, of the two possible explanations: the first, that there was a remarkable continuity of tradition extending over two hundred years and, the second, that it was indeed built at the same time, one would have to say that the plausibility of the second is far more likely. That the inscriptions on the building faithfully reflect the 7th century sacred Islamic beliefs is not surprising since inscriptions are easily added to an existing building. Sauvaget writes of a similarity between the mosaics and decorations of the Medina and Cordoba mosques but Khoury cautions that the Cordoba mosque had no decorations until the Al-Hakam expansion and that the description of the Medina mosque in Arabia comes to us at a later date. Perhaps the similarity of decoration is exaggerated or, if there is a correspondence, it can be explained by the common Near East sources of both buildings.

5

Orientation and Form

What are the main characteristics of the Mosque of Cordoba that would have served the functions required by Islam or by the Phoenicians? To begin, let us examine the key question of mosque orientation. Unlike the many requirements of a cathedral, a mosque can take many forms. But it must have at least one mihrab and that mihrab must orient to Mecca. It was Mohammad who ordered that the orientation in prayer of the believer must be shifted from facing Jerusalem to facing Mecca. The physical place of worship need only be a prayer mat in the desert. Then why is it that perhaps half the medieval mosques of the world do not face Mecca? David A. King, Arabist and mathematician, makes it quite clear that the medieval mosque frequently did not face Mecca:

> The world of Islam has always centered on the holy city of Mecca, or, more precisely on the Kaaba, the sacred sanctuary there. Wherever Muslims have settled they have faced the Kaaba in prayer, and all mosques are supposed to face that direction. But hundreds of medieval mosques, scattered from Andalusia to Central Asia, are not properly aligned towards Mecca. Some face due south, whether Mecca lies in that direction or not; *the Great Mosque of Cordova in Spain faces the deserts of Algeria rather than those of Arabia* (my italics); various mosques in Syria and Turkey face southwest rather than southeast; and some mosques in Central Asia face due west rather than southwest. (David A. King, *"Faces of the Kaaba"*, p. 17)

King has argued that this basic requirement was often set aside in a community in order to respect local traditions of orientation of sacred buildings. While this is a logical answer it runs counter to the prime requisite of all mosques, medieval or contemporary. In total ignorance or disregard of this evidence of massive non-orientation, a candidate for a Doctor of Philosophy at Pennsylvania State University in 2000 AD makes the blanket statement:

> All mosques in the world are oriented in the same direction, facing the Holy Kabah in Makkah. (Mohammed A. Alomar, <u>History, Theory and Belief: A Conceptual Study of the Traditional Mosque in Islamic Architecture</u>, p. 98)

The belief that all mosques, medieval and contemporary, face Mecca is so ingrained in the thinking of intellectuals concerned with Islamic architecture that even a recent graduate cannot conceive of it being otherwise. Nor did his thesis advisers nor the publishers seem to be aware or concerned. But this is far from the truth with regards to medieval mosques.

The Mosque of Cordoba faces 60 degrees south of east whereas Mecca is 10 degrees 14 minutes south of east from Cordoba. Thus, the building orients about 50 degrees away from Mecca. Obviously, there could not have been any intent to align the building's axis towards Mecca. It has been argued that by being oriented more or less to the south it was duplicating the relationship of Mecca to Medina thereby recreating a holy alignment; some hold that this may have been a local preference of the mullahs in the 8th century AD. Maria Rosa Menocal, professor at Yale University whose focus is medieval culture especially the mixed cultures of Spain, argues in <u>The Ornament of the World</u> that the building faces south (sic!) because it was intended to replicate the orientation of Damascus to Mecca. She asserts that the wish to build a second Mosque of Damascus in Spain was psychologically so overwhelming that the new mosque was given a southerly orientation. She offers no evidence for this conjecture. Considering the importance of the building and the renowned ability of the famous Islamic astronomers at that time to determine directions accurately, it is highly unlikely that it was simply an oversight. In any case, it does not orient south but 30 degrees east of south. Likewise, the Mosque at Qairouan in Tunisia orients approximately southeast whereas the true direction of Mecca from Qairouan is 20 degrees 43 minutes south of east.

The Mosque of Cordoba and the Mosque of Qairouan are both trapezoidal shaped. The Mosque at Qairouan is 214' on its north side, 230' on its south side, 396' on its east side and 395' on its west side (Creswell, Early Muslim Architecture, p. 251). Were both buildings meant to be similar in shape to the Kaaba? According to Creswell, the Kaaba is 22 cubits on its north side, 20 cubits on its south side, 32 cubits on its east side and 31 cubits on its west side. Can we know the true dimensions of the Kaaba before its various restorations?

The design of sacred buildings in the Phoenician realm did not seem to follow the typical model of sacred building orientations of ancient times, including those of India and China, which favored the cardinal directions. Thus, with regards to orientation the door is open for a Phoenician influence or origin of some ancient monuments which do not respect the orientation traditions of Islam, China or India.

The problem of a sacred building of Islam not facing Mecca is also evident in the Taj Mahal in Agra, India. Though allegedly built in the 17th century by the emperor Shah Jahan of the Moghul dynasty and incorporating a mosque as part of its complex, the complex orients to the cardinal directions. The alleged mosque, which is due west of the central Taj building, therefore faces due west. But Mecca is not due west of Agra. It is westerly, actually 12 degrees south of west. The whole complex when planned could have been tipped twelve degrees to enable the mosque to have its correct Mecca orientation. But this was not done. Therefore, one must question whether the mosque originally functioned as a mosque and, therefore, whether the Taj complex was built by Islam. There are many other alleged Islamic buildings in the world that require innovative study to test their real origins.

The second most troublesome anomaly of the Mosque of Cordoba is the theory that it was built in four stages over two hundred years from 786 AD to 1007 AD. First, from the viewpoint of planning, the completion of Stage III by Hakham II in 976 A.D. would have resulted, if it was actually an addition, in an elongated building running roughly from north to south with the mihrab at the south end. The problem is that it is extremely rare, perhaps non-existent, to have a mosque whose prayer hall is elongated along its axis which is perpendicular to the mihrab. If the shape of Stage III were actually shaped as the scholars tell us, it would have been awkward for listeners and viewers to experience the imam on the mimbar adjacent to the mihrab from which he gave his orations. Second, if there were an intent to build the mosque in stages to suit a growing community, it would have made more sense to have started with the first stage to the south and build subsequent stages to the north so that the highly decorated mihrab and adjacent rooms in each stage would have been spared repeated demolition.

The third consideration that mitigates against the concept of stages is the apparent absence of construction joints in the exterior wall between the supposed four stages. A careful examination of what would have been the stone interfaces between the various stages reveals no discontinuity of construction. The elevation of the exterior southwest wall in the photo below shows the absence of any discontinuity in masonry construction (Pl.Va). Instead, the ashlar stone blocks overlap in a saw-tooth manner as is to be expected in a continuous, integrated wall. While it is true that over time and allowing for subsequent replacement of materials, and with the addition of layers of finishing materials, the joints may have become concealed. But in all visible locations the exposed stone shows no break in the interlocking of the stonework and no discontinuity in the overlapping stone pattern. This lack of evidence was checked in several places around the perimeter of the enclosing wall with invariable similar results. Until there is a closer examination of the construction of the walls at their critical points of discontinuity one must maintain a very skeptical attitude regarding the four stage theory.

6

Astronomical Correlations

One of the most fascinating aspects of the plan of the Mosque of Cordoba is its astronomical correlations, yet scholars have failed to investigate this even though I published my findings ten years ago. As we noted earlier, the mosque faces 60 degrees south of east along its central axis. Is it by coincidence that the southwest side of the Kaaba in Mecca also faces in the same direction? The Mosque of Cordoba is a quadrilateral but not quite a rectangle. Its four sides are unequal and its northeast side is not parallel to its southwest side. The Kaaba is also a quadrilateral but not a rectangle (Fig. VIa). Was the mosque meant to be similar in form or relate spatially to the Kaaba? There is nothing in the Islamic medieval literature to suggest that a geometrically parallel relationship was purposefully arranged. The mosque's appropriate Islamic orientation would have been, of course, to face the Kaaba rather than be parallel to it.

The Kaaba's exact original dimensions are not known. Its geodetic relationship to Egypt is interesting in that Egypt's west boundary is at 39 degrees 50 minutes East longitude while Cordoba's longitude, according to the Oxford Atlas of the World, is at 4 degrees 50 minutes West longitude. This makes for exactly 43 degrees of difference. Is this precision a coincidence?

Let us examine a possible common purpose between the Mosque of Cordoba, Stonehenge in England and the Kaaba. Gerald Hawkins, in his memorable research on Stonehenge in England, has proven Stonehenge to be a pre-historic computer designed to tally the three metonic cycles of the lunar winter solstice of 18.61 years which add up closely to 56. The 56 Aubrey holes arranged in a circle at Stonehenge I served as a counter of the lunar winter solstices:

> The nodes of the moon's orbit regresses around the ecliptic ... 18.61 average tropical years. (Gerald S. Hawkins, Beyond Stonehenge, p. 301)

He explains that 18.61 years is the time interval for the moon to return to the extreme azimuths on the horizon at the winter and summer solstices and that the best integer is three of these groups of years to add up to almost exactly 56. Therefore, the Aubrey circle was designed as a computer device for predicting the year in which the moon will reach its extreme azimuth.

Stonehenge is exactly 30 degrees west of the western boundary of Ancient Egypt which had a longitude of 29 degrees 50 minutes East, while Stonehenge is 1 degree 50 minutes West. Was the longitude of Stonehenge purposefully set to relate to ancient Egypt? Apparently, its latitude was selected to satisfy various astronomical needs including the prediction of eclipses while maintaining a precise 40 degree tilt to its axis.

David King has demonstrated that the Kaaba, too, has astronomical observatory capabilities based on a modern plan of the Kaaba taken from a map of Mecca prepared from aerial photographs:

> ... the minor axis ... is precisely aligned toward the southernmost setting position of the moon at the winter solstice, over the hills to the southwest of Mecca. This discovery was made a few years ago by Gerald Hawkins, best known for his work on the alignments of Stonehenge, which he conducted in the 1960s.
>
> Roughly every nineteen years, the crescent moon sets at the spot on the horizon visible along the southeast side of the Kaaba. This lunar alignment is also found in many megalithic sites in Europe. There is no mention of this specific lunar alignment in the medieval Islamic texts on folk astronomy.... *This lunar alignment of the Kaaba may well have been intentional"*(my italics). (David A. King, *"Faces of the Kaaba"*, p.20)

It is believed by Tompkins that the Kaaba, since it long preceded the Islamic era, was of geodetic significance to the Near East. It may be that it was well known to the Phoenicians who for some reason considered it a sacred site, honored its existence and identified the Kaaba with the warehouse/temple that they built at Cordoba. While the size of the Kaaba was much smaller, the form and orientation may both have been similar. Siting along the southeast wall of the Kaaba one can observe the crescent moon setting over the west end of the southeast wall at the winter solstice. The location of the Kaaba in the desert in Arabia must have been chosen so that this phenomenon could occur, while at the same time the southeast wall was built extending from 30 degrees north of east to 30 degrees south of west. Why this particular angle was considered important is not known. We are also informed by Thompson that the longitudinal location of the Kaaba is exactly 10 degrees east of the eastern boundary of ancient Egypt.

With similar purposefulness, the location of the Mosque of Cordoba must have been selected at a point up the Guadalquivir River where at the same angle of orientation as the Kaaba it also offers a significant astronomical orientation. In this case, the orientation of the Mosque of Cordoba is to the sun so that at the summer solstice the sun sets on the west horizon over the southeast wall:

> Assuming the wall is at Azimuth 60 degrees, and the skyline is flat, then the declination is 22.9 degrees. The sun would, today, stand approximately on that line at the summer solstice, being one diameter above the flat horizon. You can interpolate for dates in between. (Hawkins, Letter to Mills)

In the case of both buildings, specific geographical locations were chosen to enable the buildings to investigate celestial relationships while maintaining specified orientations. The Kaaba's south-east wall orients to the moon's winter solstice every 18.61 years with an accuracy of closer than one degree. Since the Mosque of Cordoba is in a completely different latitude and longitude, the same astronomical relationship obviously could not pertain. The mosque may have other celestial relationships that we are not yet aware of. Future research may reveal even more interesting phenomena.

Tracking the sequence of months until the moon returns completely to its original position in the heavens takes 56 months. The three part sequence of 19, 19, 18 months was accounted for at Stonehenge when the Aubrey pit circle of 56 positions was revealed by Hawkins to be a means of counting the months so that one could anticipate the moon's complete return at the 56th month. At Cordoba there are 18 bays and 19 piers on the exterior southeast wall (Fig. VIb). By placing a marker at an appropriate place at the wall and moving it each month, the Phoenicians could, after three successive turns, arrive at the final position. There is no proof that this was the intent of the architects. Yet, in ancient times, where symbolism counted so heavily, very little was built arbitrarily. Astronomical considerations counted heavily, as we know from the pyramids (Tompkins) and the Temple at Karnak. If the walls were built as an aid to reading the heavens then this would be another reason for suggesting that the four stages of the Mosque of Cordoba were actually all built at one time—but only as far as the exterior walls are concerned. The current assumption that the exterior wall's northeast side was completed with the final addition in the fourth stage of construction by Al Mansur would then negate the moon marker possibility by reducing the number of piers to 12 instead of 19.

The unexpected orientation of the Mosque of Cordoba has been noted by David King, a mathematician and analyst of mosque orientations:

> Wherever Muslims have settled they have faced the Kaaba in prayer, and all mosques are supposed to face that direction. But hundreds of medieval mosques, scattered from Andalusia to Central Asia, are not properly aligned toward Mecca. Some face due south, whether Mecca lies in that direction or not; the Great Mosque of Cordoba in Spain faces the deserts of Algeria rather than those of Arabia; various mosques in Syria and Turkey face southwest rather than southeast; and some mosques in Central Asia face due west rather than southwest. (King, *"Faces of the Kaaba"*, p.17)

The mosque does not face Mecca and it is in fact parallel along its longitudinal axis with the southwest wall of the Kaaba. The Kaaba, he says, was purposely oriented to the crescent setting moon as the moon completed its

19 year metonic cycle and would be seen again along the south-east wall in the same place on the horizon. This minor axis of the Kaaba:

> ... is precisely aligned toward the southernmost setting position of the moon at the winter solstice, over the hills to the southwest of Mecca. (King, *"Faces of the Kaaba"*, p. 20)

King also attributes a relationship of the Kaaba along its major north-west/south-east axis to the rising star Canopus, the brightest star in the southern heavens. There may indeed be multiple astronomical relationships intentionally built into the Kaaba but none of them are acknowledged in the scriptures of Islam. We know that the Kaaba is pre-Islamic. Perhaps then the Mosque of Cordoba, with its as yet unacknowledged astronomical relationships, is also pre-Islamic. King puts to rest any conjecture on our part that perhaps the Muslims at the time of the building of the Mosque of Cordoba in the late 8th century, did not have the knowledge of how to orient a building. He says:

> The world's leading mathematicians and astronomers from the eighth century to perhaps the fourteenth century were Muslims, and the determination of the qibla was one of their favorite problems. To find it, one needs to know the latitude and longitude of one's own city, and of Mecca, and a formula to calculate the qibla from these coordinates. Muslim astronomers devised both geometric and trigonometric solutions to the problem. They compiled lists of localities and the direction to Mecca from each locality, and even adopted universal solutions to the qibla problem: tables displaying the qibla for each degree of latitude and longitude, computed with remarkable accuracy. After the fourteenth century, qibla boxes containing a magnetic compass and engraved with lists of localities and their qiblas, came into common use.
>
> In short, within two centuries after the death of Muhammad, Muslim astronomers could compute the qibla for any locality in the Muslim world. As a result many mosques were erected with their prayer halls facing Mecca precisely. But medieval Muslim scientists, following Hellenistic traditions of mathematical geography, were at odds intellectually with the tenets of Islam. And it seems that in the medieval world,

few people listened to astronomers, least of all religious scholars, whose opinions tended to regulate popular practice. These scholars had their own ideas about qibla determination, although inevitably differences of opinion arose. (King, *"Faces of the Kaaba"*, p. 18)

Perhaps King's views on the capability of the Muslims to orient buildings to Mecca allows for a period of astronomical immaturity at the inception of the Mosque of Cordoba since the two centuries of developing expertise had not quite elapsed before the mosque was allegedly begun. But his conjecture that Muslim scholars and geographical mathematicians may have been at odds with one another does not seem convincing. Why would the religious leaders have defied that injunction?

King conjectures that the Mosque of Cordoba may have been built with a qibla orientation purposefully parallel to the Kaaba rather than facing it. This seems an unwarranted assumption since he admits that the many associations of the mosque with the Kaaba are known to us through medieval texts and this is not one of them. Even if they did exist they may be merely commentaries to support prevalent Islamic attitudes and practices. The real answer to King's conjectures and tortuous speculations were in front of him but he could not cope with a new overview. He realizes that:

> Occasionally, of course, mosques were built on the sites of churches and pagan temples, without modification of the orientation of the earlier edifices."(King, *Astronomical Alignments in Medieval Islamic Religious Architecture*, p. 304)

He stops short of saying that the early mosques may have been appropriated from other cultures and religions and that explains their alternative qibla orientations.

There may have been some calendar significance to the number of bays in the first three stages of the mosque, which were probably, in fact, built in one construction period. There would have been, then, 11 aisles or naves and 33 cross-aisles giving a total of 363 bays. If we count the two bays of the minaret we have 365—the solar days in a year. Did each bay represent one day in the year? Was the building built in two stages rather than four: the first stage comprising what we now consider the first three stages and the complete exterior wall; the real second stage being the interior rework of Phase IV of al-Mansur, prime minister of Hisham II (976-1013)?

Or there may have been only 360 unobstructed bays in the original Phoenician hypostyle hall if one does not count the altar for the god (later the mihrab), the altar's two adjacent bays and the two bays of the minaret. Then the total of clear bays would have come to 360. This could have been intended to represent the number of days in the lunar year. By moving a marker each day to the adjacent bay the Phoenicians could have remained aware of the progress of the lunar year.

On the interior it seems more likely that the columns, arches and roof that make up Stage IV were probably later additions by the Muslims. A test of the voussoirs of the arches in Stage IV revealed that they were not made up of alternating red brick and white stone but that the arches were made of stone covered with stucco and painted. By drilling into the apparent brick it became clear to me that they were not indeed that material when the loosened stucco rained down.

The plan of the layout of the columns in Stage IV also show that the original spacing between columns is not maintained in all spacing between the third and fourth stages. Here, then, is evidence of discontinuity which could be indicative of a later addition. But the exterior walls, as mentioned earlier, show no such discontinuity. What seems more likely is that a Phoenician courtyard area on the northeast side was converted to a mosque extension by Al Mansur. (See Fig. VIb for my conception of what the original area may have looked like.)

The largest part of the prayer hall could have been used for storage of grain and wine which were kept cool by the circulation of air from the lower level beneath the main floor and grilles that are still apparent in the exterior walls. The area confronting the mihrab near the southeast wall was probably used as the Phoenician temple and audience hall. The supposedly later mihrab may have been used originally as a niche for the god of commerce of the Phoenicians—Melqart.

Normally, there are two shapes for mihrab niches in medieval mosques: either rectangular or dished. To have a niche that is in itself a room is not typical. The niche only represents a sacred presence and a sacred direction. It was never meant to be a space that one entered. Since there would never be a representation of Allah there or anywhere, there would be no need for a room. Yet this is precisely what we have here—a small room. The space is eight-sided counting the open end towards the maqsura. Each side is about 7' long. Its octagon shape suggests a Hindu inspiration representing, in Hindu temple orientation, the four cardinal directions and the intermediate directions. Above the space of the mihrab, the ceiling is in the form of a conch shell. The conch is one of the attributes of Vishnu. He is often depicted holding a conch in one of his several hands. We know little about the ways that the Phoenicians may have been influenced by Vedic culture but Vedic culture spread over a large area and may have ultimately influenced Phoenician Spain. This form of the mihrab as a room-sized niche became a model for later mihrabs in Spain and North Africa.

The heavy metals—gold, silver, tin and copper—were probably kept on the lower level so as not to overburden the first level floor. The search for precious metals was perhaps the greatest source of the drive for commercial gain as the Phoenicians sent their ships to the far end of the Mediterranean and beyond to the Cornwall area of England in their quest for tin. Having refined the metals and converted them to slabs they were perhaps stored in the basement of the warehouse. Since the structure was built on a downward slope to the river, the metals from the lower level could be readily moved out through openings in the southeast wall and moved directly to the ships waiting in the harbor to be loaded—or, as a component of trade, products may have been taken from the ships to the warehouse to be stored. The need to guard the high value of the metals would account for the fortified nature of the building—its piers, thick walls and crenellations.

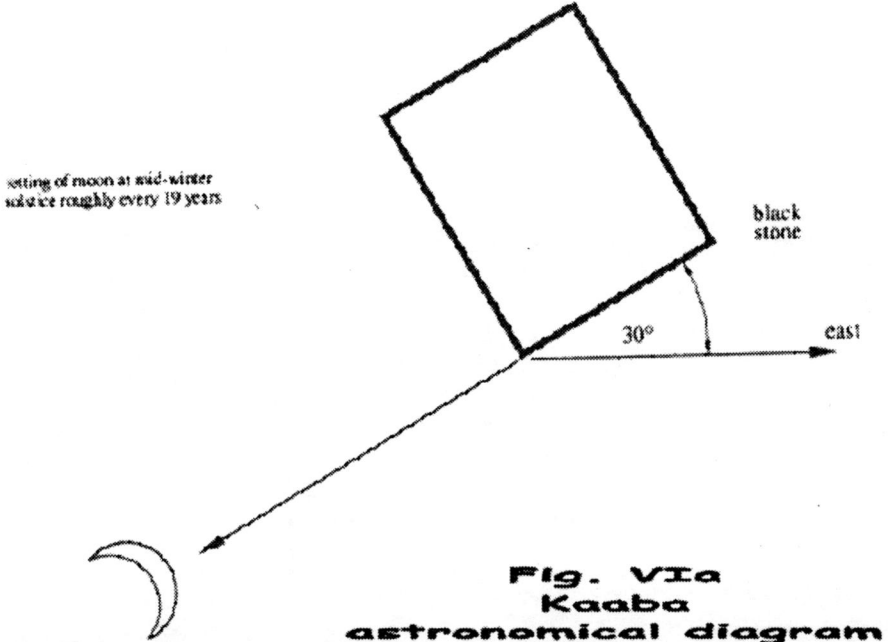

Fig. VIa
Kaaba
astronomical diagram

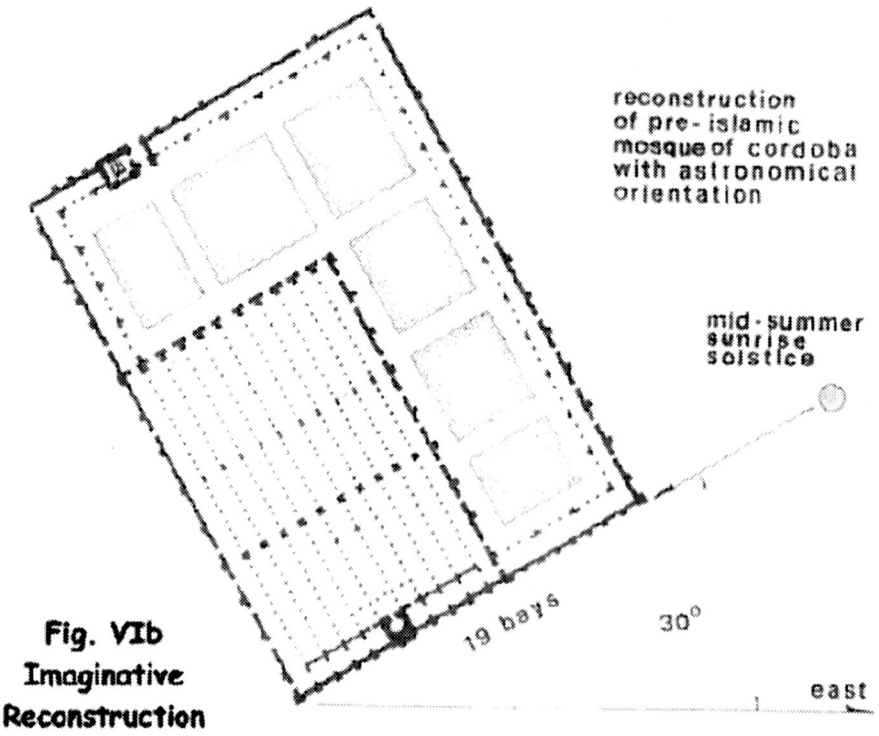

Fig. VIb
Imaginative
Reconstruction

7

Time to Construct

The theory of a Roman origin of the Mosque of Cordoba was compelling for me at first because of the apparent unreliability of the prevalent paradigm of the development of Islamic art and architecture concerning the origin of the Mosque of Cordoba. In addition to the absence of contemporary historical data and the unfavorable social conditions in the early Umayyad period for producing massive, elegant construction, one must consider that certain architectural and decorative features associated with the mosque had virtually no precedent prior to Islamic Spain, nor had there ever been a mosque of that scale, and it is doubtful that the Arab and Berber invaders, mostly nomadic peoples, were capable of producing anything in Spain on the technical level of the Mosque of Cordoba. Furthermore, there is no evidence of a crescendo of development leading up to its construction nor was there any spread of construction works by the community beyond the ruling dynasty during and following the mosque's completion.

An additional reason to question the reliability of the Arab sources and subsequent promoters of that traditional explanation is the short span of time various scholars allow for the construction of the mosque's large Stage I construction in 786. In the beginning, we are told, an existing Christian church was demolished to make way for the prayer hall which was said to be 79 meters wide by 42 meters deep, covering 3,330 square meters. In addition, there were 1,590 square meters of courtyard. The prayer hall was the largest of any mosque built in the West at the time, yet al-Razi asserts that the construction was completed in one year, and al-Makkari suggests that it took two years. G. T. Rivoira denies that one year is a possibility:

It has been maintained, on the words of Arabic writers, that the founder did not make much change in the appearance of the Christian building, and that the mosque was erected within the year 786; *an idea not in accordance either with the possibilities of construction, or historical facts (*my italics*)*. On the death of Abd al-Rahman I in 788, the operations which he had contemplated were unfinished; and the two years or more of work, pushed on as we know it was, they cannot have gone further than the erection of the mosque proper. And we cannot even imagine that this happened, if we consider that the five years required for Hisham's completion of the building are too much for merely constructing the cloistered court and the minaret on the north side of the mosque. The period of eight years (from 786 to 793) is the same as that which the mosque of Damascus, the source of inspiration for that of Cordova, demanded from Walid for the full expansion of its beauty (706-714). (Rivoira, Moslem Architecture, pp. 363-364)

Elie Lambert, however, asserts even more vigorously that it would have taken closer to fifteen years to complete a hall of that size, arguing that the extension (Stage II) by Abd ar-Rahman II, which was shallower, took fifteen years to complete even though he had more expert builders at his disposal:

> Un premier fait assez étrange parait ressortir de cette histoire. A l'époque d'Abd er-Rahman Ier, ou l'art de bâtir était encore assez rudimentaire dans l'Islam d'Occident, un an a peine aurait suffi pour réaliser le projet conçu par l'emir omeyiyade de construire une mosquée a l'instar de celle que ses peres avaient elevées a Damas et pour edifier en entrer un oratoire de plus de 3,000 metres carrés: d'après le Bayan en effet, en l'an 169 de l'Hegire (785) Abd er-Rahman Ier commença la demolition de l'Église et des 170 la construction était achevée. Sous Abd er-Rahman II, au contraire, il aurait fallu plus de quinze années pour agrandir simplement cette salle de prières sur un profundeur sensiblement moindre.(Lambert, Études Medievales, p. 55) *(A rather basic strange fact emerges from this history. In the epoch of Abd ar-Rahman I, when the art of building was still rather rudimentary in western Islam, one year would have hardly sufficed to accomplish the project conceived by the Ummayad emir to construct a mosque similar to what is forefathers had built in Damascus and to build as one entered an oratory of more than*

3,000 square meters: according to Bayan, in the year 169 of the Hegira (7850 Abd ar-Rahman I began the demolition of the Church and by 170 the construction was complete. Under Abd ar-Rahman II, on the other hand, it took more than fifteen years to simply enlarge the prayer hall with a smaller depth.")

This is a keen observation by Lambert but, unfortunately, he comes to an unlikely conclusion. He reasons that Stage I was too complex to have been built in such a short time and, therefore, the building must have then had a lower ceiling and been carried on simple arches. Evidence for this is lacking. The sophisticated, double-arch and forest of columns design of the prayer hall is basic to the concept of the building.

All this vagueness and conjecture should make us wonder whether the estimates of rapid construction are not all mistakes or fabrications. On the other hand, remodeling of an existing building could have been done comfortably in the year or two cited by the two Arab historians. Thus, from the point of view of practicality of de novo construction time, the suggested times of construction do not hold up. They are only reasonable if interpreted as modifications of an existing structure.

8

The Lady Vanishes

How can we account for the provenance of the beautiful and mysterious stone sculpture known as Our Lady of Elche or La Dama de Elche. The Dama de Elche was discovered in 1897 near the Valencian town of Elche in southeast Spain close to the Mediterranean. It is made of limestone and is 22 inches high. It was spirited away to the Louvre in Paris where it stayed for more than forty years and came back to Spain after an agreement between Vichy France and Franco in 1941.

Scholars vary in their conjectures from dismissing it completely as an unaccountable anomaly to accepting it as indigenous or Phoenician. The Spaniards out of pride and patriotism are mostly agreed that it is genuine, representing early Iberian, Punic and indigenous character and favoring a date of origin from between the 5th century and 3rd century BC. All concerned realize that there are only vague clues to the significance of its special characteristics. It is a fine statue in excellent condition. The woman has an elaborate headdress with unique circular ear adornments almost as large as her head. She wears three rows of necklaces. A mantle is draped across her shoulders. She has a proud and serene bearing. The back of the statue has an opening intended to hold some object. This same feature is evident in a similar second statue known as the Dama de Baza which was found in the necropolis of Baza near Granada in a grave that also contained pottery and jewelry.

Both may be Atlantean. Relating the two statues to Phoenician sources can only be guesswork since we do not know of other statues from Phoenicia that share these characteristics. La Dama de Elche statue and another of related vintage called the Dama de Cerro de los Santos, can be found in Room 20 of the Museo Archaeologico Nacional in Madrid, according to

Julie Skurdenis, a journalist, writing in "Focus on Archaeology" in International Travel News, July 2001.

The Atlanteans were, if we accept their existence, probably in part at least, composed of fair-skinned people. They could have been related to the fair-skinned Lady of Elche. The legends of the Indians of Mexico and Peru being visited by fair people who taught them many things about agriculture, science and government and then departed may have referred to peoples from Atlantis whose influence extended out in all directions. In the Footprints of the Gods, Graham Hancock says that the defeat of the Aztecs was hastened by their belief that the Spanish were returning gods who had visited them earlier and whom they believed would one day return, and that those people were fair-skinned with advanced technological and scientific knowledge. This belief gave the Spanish an awesome advantage which enabled them to mollify the resistance of the Indians.

The Olmecs, though a technologically advanced people, were among the earliest, civilizations of Mexico, dating back at least to 1200 BC, though Zapp would date them much earlier. The Aztecs and Mayans borrowed much of their cultures from them. Their civilization shows no early progressive development. Like the Mosque of Cordoba, their advanced engineering works and remarkable 20 ton Negroid sculptured heads also seem to have no precedent. The Negro heads discovered at La Venta could be much older than the accompanying carbon-dated fragments from which they were dated at 1200 BC. In my judgment, the heads seem to be racially related to the peoples of Southeast Asia.

But there were other sculptures, of white men, discovered in Latin-America. Graham Hancock describes the excavation by the famous American archaeologist Mathew Stirling in 1940:

> Sterling and his team worked for two days to free the great rock. When exposed it proved to be an imposing stele fourteen feet high, seven feet wide and almost three feet thick. The carvings showed an encounter between two tall men, both dressed in elaborate robes and wearing elegant shoes with turned-up toes. Either erosion or deliberate mutilation (quite commonly practiced on Olmec monuments) had resulted in the complete defacement of one of the figures. The other was intact. It so

obviously depicted a *Caucasian male* (my italics) with a high-bridged nose and a long, flowing beard that the bemused archaeologists promptly christened it 'Uncle Sam'. (Hancock, <u>Fingerprints of the Gods</u>, p. 133)

Hancock brings to our attention that there have been researchers who speculated that the bearded white men might have been Phoenicians who sailed through the Pillars of Hercules at the Straits of Gibraltar and across the Mediterranean in the second millenium BC and that the Negro heads were slaves from west Africa that the Phoenicians had picked up prior to crossing the Atlantic. He rejects the possibility that the Negroes were slaves since their demeanor in the sculpture is proud and aristocratic, not servile. He rejects the Phoenician origin thesis on stylistic grounds arguing that there is nothing in the Olmec sites that suggests Phoenician handiwork, and that from a stylistic point of view these powerful works seemed to belong to no known culture and are without precedent.

Hancock argues from analogy with ancient Egypt that there must have been a third party. Just as the hieroglyphics and the Great Pyramids and Sphinx show no pre-dynastic roots, so in the Olmec sites the Caucasian men must have been the outside source. While the Egyptian civilization leaps to greatness about 3000 BC, the Olmec civilization does not suddenly emerge until 1500 BC. What happened in those 1500 years—assuming a third party was responsible for both? The answer, he suggests, is that some unknown setback delayed the emergence in Mexico. In fact, the giant stone heads and the reliefs of bearded men could have originated in Central America at the time of Egypt's emergence and been saved and brought forward again in 1500 BC. Hancock believes that there was a now lost continent in the Pacific from which people of an advanced civilization traveled to both Egypt and Central America bestowing their advanced technology and science to promote advanced civilizations in Pyramid Egypt and Olmec Mexico.

Perhaps the Lady of Elche was also an Atlantean figure. Being an enigma to researchers, it is usually dropped from books on early Spain in order to avoid speculation that fits no paradigm. Her features do not seem to be Near Eastern. Her large spiral "earmuffs" do not suggest some known ethnic derivation.

In his argument against the Lady of Elche called "Art Forgery: The Case of the Lady of Elche", written in 1995, the American art historian John F. Moffitt reasons that the practically pristine sculpture was found in an area that had only fragments of remains which he considers highly suspicious; that the soil around the bust was loose when it should normally have been compacted; that the facial characteristics are neither classical Greek nor Roman nor Iberian; that Spanish nationalism has created a will to believe; and that there is a climate of other forgeries of which this is a part.

He attributes the "forgery" to an accomplished sculptor who was probably influenced by the symbolist movement in painting and sculpture. Thus the languid look, the droopy eyelids are not unlike sculpture used for cemeteries at that time. Drawings that were available at the time were interpreted to supply the necklaces, "earmuffs" and clothing. He argues that any forger can only see his artwork through the prevailing criteria for beauty of his time. It belongs, says Moffitt, in a museum of modern contemporary art being in itself of artistic merit.

Unfortunately, Moffitt considers only two possibilities of origin: Punic or late 19th century. An Atlantean provenance responds to some problems intrinsic to the limitation of these two choices. The curious and sophisticated characteristics of the lady can be explained by their being of another and advanced culture. The lack of racial and ethnic affinities can be explained by its being representative of a different people. Its resemblance to other finds in the area that are considered genuine shows that it was not just a unique invention by a much later forger but a very successful instance of a body of typical figures. Its clarity, elegance and sophistication are on the level of the achievements by the same people who produced the architecture of the Mosque of Cordoba, the Alhambra and Medina Azahara.

9

Heavenly Arches

Henri Terrasse raises some interesting questions regarding the distinctive superimposed double arches in the prayer hall of the Mosque of Cordoba. The innovative architect, whoever he was, found a way to raise the ceiling height without using large columns, which would be difficult to obtain, or without adding visually disturbing horizontal beams for bracing. He doubled the arches such that the upper arch was semi-circular and the lower arch was horseshoe shaped. The upper arch supported the roof. The lower arch braced the otherwise too long vertical columns. The inventiveness of the unknown architect was magnificent. The combination of structural performance and esthetic delight is superb. There were some applications of the horseshoe arch in use in Spain during and preceding the Visigothic period. But there is no accepted precedent in the Near East or in Spain for this type of internal structural arrangement of the double arch. Ernest T. Dewald, professor at Cooper Union in New York and specialist in Italian art, concludes concerning the pre-Islamic existence of the horseshoe arch in Spain:

> ... that the appearance of the horseshoe arch in western Europe is due directly to influences from Syria and Asia Minor, carried by Eastern colonists to the West. That in Spain, it survived into the Visigothic period along with other Eastern motives of late Roman art, and became a well-known feature in the art of that country at that time, existing side by side with the semicircular arch as it had in Syria. (*"The Appearance of the Horseshoe Arch in Western Europe"*, American Journal of Archaeology, 1922, p. 330)

He disagrees with Holland who asserted that that the Moors introduced the horseshoe arch in Spain and provides many examples in both Syria and Spain. The issue that Dewald neglects to take up by limiting his search to churches in Syria is how far back in time could the horseshoe arch be dated to. How did it get to Syria and Asia Minor? Could its appearance in both Syria and Spain be attributed to a common source that was developed in the Phoenician era?

The horseshoe arch was used in the rock-cut temples of India before Islam began. Though these were not structural they reflected other uses which did not survive where they were probably structural. Super-imposed arches were used at Ctesiphon built by the Parthians near the city of Baghdad, and in the Roman bridges in Spain. But Lambert has some questions about the ability of the Muslims to have produced the elaborate multi-foil arches in the maqsura area in front of the mihrab:

> Tous ces arcs sont paramentés selon la manière des Goths: ni les Musulmans, ni les Chrétiens n'eussent eté capables de les élever dans un style aussi artistique et aussi délicat. (Lambert, p. 74) *(All these arches are fashioned according to the Gothic style: neither the Muslims nor the Christians were capable of raising them in a style as artistic and delicate.)*

By "Goths" he may have been alluding to the Visigoths. It is not clear.

The multi-foil arch was used as a variation of the double arches to great effect in the maqsura area in front of the mihrab of the Mosque of Cordoba. The magnificent baroque shapes are startling and festive. Rivoira accepts the concept that the multifoil arch originated in India:

> The multifoil arch has its origin in the trefoil arch first used in Gandhara as an ornamental form for the walls and domes of 'viharas', i.e. monasteries or houses of idols, and stupas or shrines to preserve relics or the memory of sacred events. This was before 600; and later it was used in construction in Kashmir, but not before the VII century. An early and remarkable instance is afforded by the temple of Martand (724-760). (Rivoira, p. 366)

Thus, both variations of a brilliant, advanced method of design were introduced in the first large scale mosque in Spain without seeming structural precedent. Where are their more tentative applications leading up to this self-confident masterful achievement? Torres Balbas makes an interesting suggestion that the brilliantly designed double arches in the prayer hall are resting on reused columns and capitals. (Torres Balbas, La Mezquita de Cordoba y las Ruinas de Madinat al-Zahra, p. 8) Why would reused pieces be matched with marvelous new arches? How do you keep the columns from being damaged in their being taken down and reemployed? How do you adjust for the various sizes in the new setting? Perhaps the columns were not reused. Because of their pre-Islamic features historians have jumped to the conclusion that they must have been reused. Or they may have been reused columns used to replace more valuable existing columns made from semi-precious or rare stones. But the explanation may be that both columns and arches are pre-Islamic. The columns may show variation in style not because they are picked at random but because the diversity of design was intentional. Their resemblance to Roman and Visigothic styles may be due to the prevalence of a Mediterranean style with ancient roots common throughout the area.

The arches are generally composed of alternating red brick and white stone voussoirs. There are examples of this in the Roman period as in the arches in the Casa del Citarista in Pompeii, Italy which dates before 79 AD (Fig. IXa). There is precedent for this in Byzantine architecture. And there is some evidence of its use in Visigothic Spain. The original tower in the Mosque of Cordoba displays alternating voussoirs (Fig. IXc). The exterior doorway of Port Diane on the northwest side shows alternating voussoirs of stone and brick (Fig. IXb). But the alternating voussoirs in the interior of Stage IV were found to be all brick with a coating of paint over seemingly alternating voussoirs to create the impression of alternating brick and stone. By drilling into the apparently stone voussoirs, just below the white thin surface of painted stucco a rain of red powder revealed that it had a brick base. This reinforces the possibility that the interior of Stage IV was a later development meant to imitate earlier construction.

The horseshoe arch was not used to any significant degree by the Romans. Yet it was essential to the structural system of internal cross-bracing of the forest of columns in the main part of the sanctuary of the Mosque of Cordoba. It was also used as decorative, blind, intersecting arched niches above some of the portals at the various entries to the mosque (Pl. IXc) and above the tower windows (Fig. IXc).

If we accept the judgment of E. B. Havell, the renowned English historian of the early 20th century, the horseshoe arch derives from India:

> It has been explained already that the Asokan arched window (fig. 17) commonly called "horseshoe" by Western writers—a form also applied to vaults and domes—was derived from the use of bent bambu, as in Bengali thatched roofs. The exquisite symbolism, inspired by the poetry of the Vedic hymns, which was read into the structural use of it, was again that of the sun and of its floral emblem the lotus or waterlily; it suggested the sun on the horizon in a cloudless sky rising or setting over sea, lake or river. As a theological symbol, therefore, it stood for Brahma, or Buddha, or Siva, and when image-worship gradually crept into the Indo-Aryan ritual the arch became the aureole of a seated figure of the divinity, the form of which was associated in the mind of the devout with the lotus leaf. The outside line of the arched opening, following the curve of a village thatched roof, took the shape of a conventionalized line of the sacred pipal—the Bodhi tree. (E. B. Havell, <u>The Ancient Medieval Architecture of India</u>, pp. 55-56)

He interprets the horseshoe arch's symbolism as relating to the Indian lotus, symbol of purity and the rising sun, the main symbol of both Hinduism and Buddhism. A related form appears in the intersecting arches of the maqsura, the privileged inner area in front of the mihrab reserved for royalty, appearing in the so-called Stage III of the Mosque of Cordoba attributed to al-Hakem II (961-976).

One could question the concept of a Phoenician origin of use of the horseshoe arch since there seems to be no extant structure accredited to the Phoenicians that displays the horseshoe arch. But one can look to the stone sculptured edifices of Cappadocia which were used in some earler manner by the Phoenicians. They display in forms and murals the horseshoe arch. These rock-cut monasteries and churches of the Cappadocia region of Turkey show the confident use of the horseshoe arch. The architecture dates reliably from mainly the 10th to 11th centuries AD. Yet we have no information as to how far back in time those forms prevailed. Nor can we be sure that they are indigenous. There is no evidence that they were derived from earlier Spanish influence. There is no extant literature from that period that gives us an answer to these questions. The dating derives from the dates written on the murals and it is assumed that excavation and murals were part of the same endeavor. The most reasonable assumption would be that the horseshoe arch is a Near East motif whose earliest origins are unclear. In a collaboration with the Instituto Internazionale di Arte a study was made of various buildings of the Byzantine era. The church of Tokali Kilise at Goreme is illustrative of the typical use of the horseshoe arch:

> Among the churches with a transverse nave—the so-called "Mesopotamian" type, which may have reached Cappadocia from its place of origin at Tur Abdin by way of Commagene—a number of examples at Goreme may be cited…. and the church at Tokali. This last is one of the largest and richest rock churches in Cappadocia: the nave, preceded by a deep atrium hewn out of an earlier church and flanked by a small apsidal basilica, with a crypt on a lower level, has a series of deep niches along the walls, breaking up and giving a sense of depth to the frescoes, which completely cover the wall surfaces. (Paulo Cuneo, "Architecture", in <u>Arts of Cappadocia</u>, p. 90)

In the interior elevation from Lyn Rodley, <u>Cave Monasteries of Byzantine Cappadocia</u>, the facade on the northeast wall has multiple horseshoe arches. One can also realize that in the three apses beyond that wall, the forms shown in plan of the spaces are also horseshoe-shaped.

The horseshoe arch may have been known by the Phoenicians. The Phoenicians in Spain may have learned it from the Tartessians. We know that the Hindus in Mamallipurum in southeast India prior to the Muslim era demonstrated their use of the horseshoe arch in their standing, solid, rock-cut temples. The Buddhist cave temples of Ajanta, built between the 1st century AD and the 8th century AD, had stupas within the caves carved out of the solid rock showing their awareness of the bulbous dome, a three-dimensional expression of the horseshoe arch. These forms were undoubtedly reflections of construction that preceded them which used both features of arch and dome. While the Romans did not use the horseshoe arch, it was known by the Byzantines. Since we know so little about the architecture of the Phoenicians and basically nothing about the architecture of the Tartessians we will have to leave open the question of the Phoenician ability to handle those forms. Remember, scholarship has been quite willing to attribute to Islam these remarkable forms without any evidence of Islam having used them earlier. It is passed off as the brilliance of their creativity. At this point in the inquiry it seems more plausible to attribute that brilliance to the Phoenicians or the Tartessians.

Pl. IXc Exterior entry on east facade

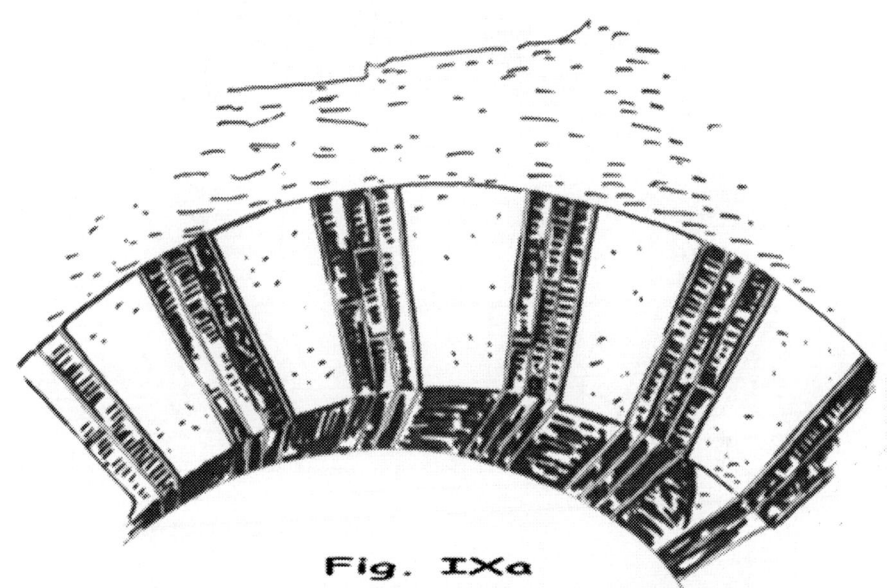

Fig. IXa
Arch in la Casa del Citarista

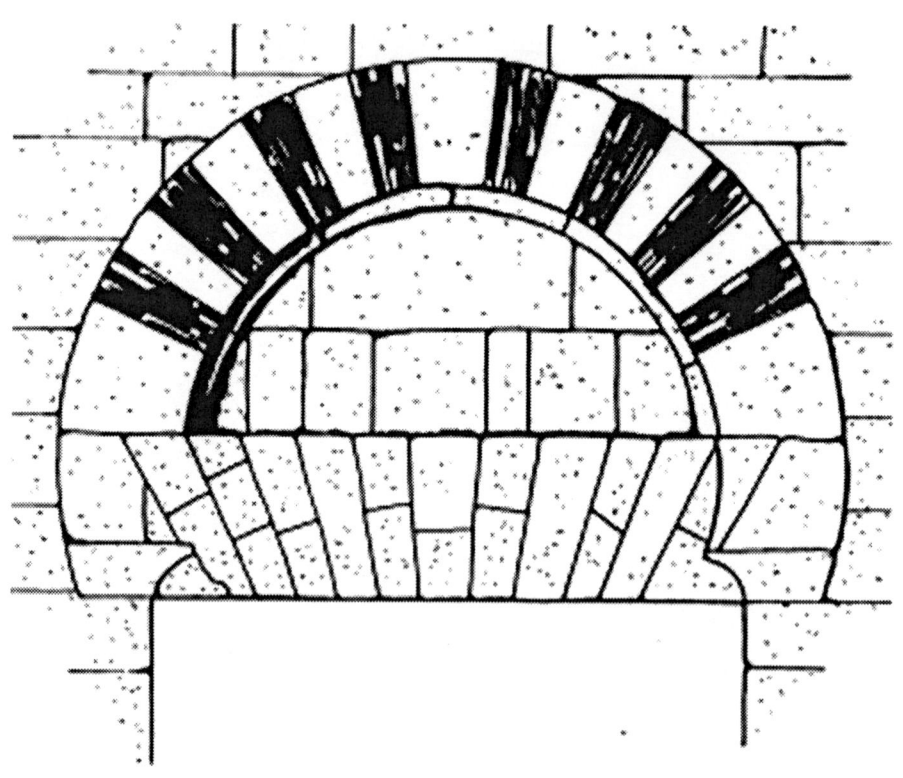

Fig. IXb
Port Diane exterior arch over doorway with alternating voussoirs

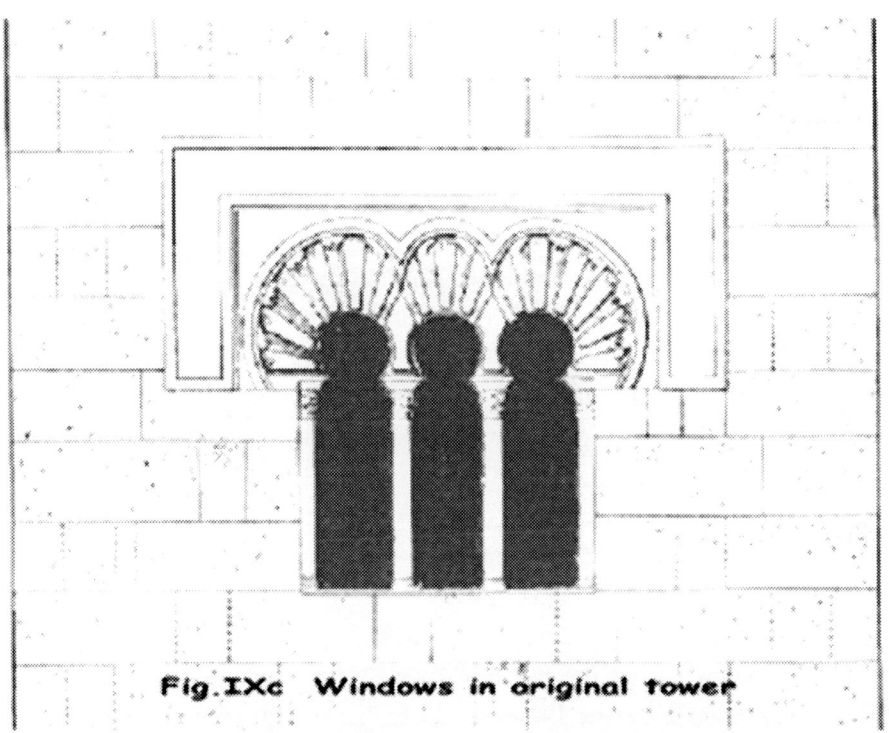

Fig.IXc Windows in original tower

10

A Most Unusual Mihrab

The mihrab in the Mosque of Cordoba has certain features that are anomalies as far as typical mosque configurations are concerned (Pl. Xa). One is first struck by the observation that it is off center from the mosque as a whole, even though it is on center with the first three stages. While it is on axis with the widest aisle, which is appropriate, one must assume that the eastern portion of the mosque is a later addition to justify the fact that the mihrab is not at the center of the whole qibla wall, the wall that theoretically should face Mecca. Since it seems likely that Stage IV was indeed a later addition, then the mihrab being off center is understandable. But it means that the later addition was built without concern for the centrality of the mihrab. The mihrab having been previously moved, it is claimed, twice before, then why the reluctance to move it again? At any rate, this off-center location must be regarded with a certain suspicion since mosques usually have a single mihrab on center. While there are extant ancient mosques with more than one mihrab, their origin must be questioned. My view is that the mihrab space in the Mosque of Cordoba was originally designed by the Phoenicians to be on center with the original hypostyle hall or "forest of columns" but became off-center when additional columns and bays were added as part of Stage IV by the Muslims at a later date. The elaborate design of the mihrab and that of the maqsura, the Muslim designation for the privileged and elaborate area reserved for the elite in front of the mihrab, with its surrounding, interlaced, lobed arches and magnificent cupolas above, were deemed to be appropriate and useful as key aspects of the mosque and were, therefore, retained (Pl. Xb).

Of special significance is the eight-sided character of the mihrab space. There are seven walls and one side opening outwards to the maqsura.

Nowhere else in previous medieval mosque construction is the mihrab designed as other than a niche, usually shaped in plan as either a curve or, infrequently, rectangular. The eight sides may relate by adaptation to the Hindu belief in the mystical importance of the eight directions. What is the connection between this mosque and Hinduism? We don't know, but in the arena of speculation that surrounds the mystery of the eight sides this explanation is as plausible as any other. The three-lobed arches in the blind niches within the mihrab are also a feature that prevailed in ancient Hindu temples perhaps symbolizing the hooded cobra. This is a room, not a niche. It probably originally contained a statue, perhaps of Melqart, the Phoenician god of commerce, to honor and protect the original commercial functions of the building.

In a remarkable stretch of the imagination, Jerrilyn Dodds, professor of architecture at City University of New York, at a loss to explain the sudden appearance of the mihrab room, opines that it was the influence of the numerous converts to Christianity and the Christian community's religious fervor that:

> ... inspired an *unconscious reactive adaptation* (my italics) of a Christian architectural form in al-Hakam II's addition, just as in the case of the tower minaret. Here this adaptation involved the space of a contemporary Mozarabic church, in particular in the three principal aisles that align with the mihrab and its ancillary doors and in the creation of the first mihrab in the history of Islam to take the form of a room. This kind of space was conceived centuries earlier to serve an ancient indigenous Christian liturgy: three longitudinal aisles and a transverse space culminating in three rooms, the central one of which can be horseshoe shaped. The Church of San Miguel de Escalada, completed in 913 (A.H. 301), provides the best parallel for this plan type. (Dodds, *"The Great Mosque of Cordoba"*, p. 21)

Thus, the three apsidal rooms of the church become forms that are adapted to the three rooms of the mosque: the treasury, the mihrab and the sabat or passageway to the palace.

She asserts that "there is no conscious allusion to Christianity here" but she is quite ready to assert the critical importance and conscious allusion of borrowed forms by the Umayyad regime which she analyzes in regard to the adaptation of the minaret. She can't have it both ways. Purposeful symbolism cannot alternate with unconscious allusion to suit scholarly explanations.

Oleg Grabar also suggests that the unusual mihrab was the result of Christian influence:

> Mais je crois que la forme de la cérémonie est empruntée au ceremonial chrétien qui existe toujours. Je crois qu'il est important, pour comprendre la psychologie qui existait à cette époque-la, comme à l'époque omeyyade à Damas, de se rappeler que le contact, la présence physique du monde chrétien était toujours là. (Grabar, *"Notes sur le Mihrab de la Grand Mosquee de Cordoue"*, p. 119). *(But I believe that the form of the ceremony was borrowed from the Christian ceremonial which always exists. I believe that it is important, to understand the psychology that existed in that epoch. As in the Ummayad epoch in Damasus, to recall that the contact, the physical presence of the Christian world was always there.)*

The mihrab ceiling is in the form of a scalloped shell. This may have, through some remote connection to Hinduism, symbolized the Indian god Vishnu, one of whose attributes is the conch shell. Since the shell is not used elsewhere in the building, nor up to that time in any other mosque, it would indicate that there was a special choice made here and, perhaps, a special symbolism. How can we entertain the possibility of Hindu influence in the building? My thesis is that we are looking back to a structure of Phoenician times that has incorporated in it cultural ties of even earlier civilizations and a wider Asian influence. There may have been an ancient Vedic influence that went well beyond the area that now constitutes India. Vedic influence and culture has been widely extirpated by both Christianity and Islam. But the stones of architecture still speak where they have been allowed to stand and call upon us to entertain new interpretations.

The mihrab form may have been derived from the niche within which the statue of the Buddha was displayed, as in the example of the stupa within the chaitya hall of Cave 19 at Ajanta in the late 5th century AD. There the Buddha is in a shallow niche between two richly carved pillars at the front of the stupa. By removing the statue and using the niche only as a sacred area it may have appeared useful as an adaptation of an existing form to Islamic liturgy without any direct recall to its former symbolism. The same transfer of forms may have occurred in Persia with the stalactites which were probably an adaptation of the multiple Buddha niches on Buddhist temples being transferred to the vault of the entrance of the mihrab.

Above the bay immediately in front of the mihrab is one of the most splendid cupolas in all of the history of architecture (Pl. Xb). The carefree springing and interlacing of vaulted beams creates a baroque type pattern in keeping with the maqsura screen wall arches and richly adorned qibla wall. Is this another example of Muslim ingenuity way ahead of its time or is it the product of an earlier culture? The jury is still out.

Bracketing the entry to the mihrab are two stone, engaged columns which are decorative, not structural. They are fashioned from two different semi-precious stone materials. Their symbolism could derive from the columns that bracket the entry to Phoenician temples and the entry to the Temple of Solomon, which was probably built by the Phoenicians. This standard design for Phoenician temples is echoed in the expression that describes the entry to the Straights of Gibraltar as the Pillars of Hercules. Both the mihrab and its columned entry, contrary to the accepted view, were there as part of the original construction and did not result from being displaced twice when Stage I was supposedly expanded to become Stage II and then Stage III. The scholars profess to having no knowledge of the form of the two supposedly previous mihrabs. Yet they are in agreement that the columns that frame the mihrab were moved from Stage II. Mercedès Lillo makes the interesting observation that the placement of the columns is unique in that instead of being up against the exterior wall, they are arranged against the jambs of the arc. She suggests that it might be fruitful to look to the Sassanids in Persia for the source of this disposition of the columns. (Lillo, *"Le Mihrab dans l'Andalus"*, p. 123)

The location of the Phoenician temple/warehouse as close to the Guadalquivir River as possible was essential to the commercial movement of materials into and out of the building. If there was any expansion at any stage in its history it would have been logically from the southeast to the northwest and not the reverse. A room in honor of Melqart, the Phoenician god of commerce, at the focal point of the building would have been appropriate. The statue of Melqart, if there was one, is long gone and its existence remains unproven but the empty room referred to as the mihrab raises some unanswered questions.

The most serious question that troubles scholars is the admittedly complete change of function of the mihrab. Instead of being not a room but a the mark of the presence of Mohammad, the chief Imam, leading the faithful to prayer and being the focal point of the orientation to Mecca, it is now a room of mystery from which no imam could comfortably emote. Had they followed their inquietude to its logical conclusion they would have entertained the idea that the mihrab was never initially intended to serve that function.

Pl. Xb Cupola in front of mihrab

11

Gargoyles and Doves

Among the many interesting features of the mosque that should be examined more closely are the gargoyles. We are told that with the return of the Christians, the Reconquista, after the conquest of Cordoba in 1013, several alterations were made to the mosque so as to change it to a cathedral. The end bays along the sidewalls in the prayer hall were converted to chapels. The bay lamps that had been bells taken from the Cathedral at Campostelo in the extreme northwest of Spain were returned to the mosque where they had originally been. One set of changes was the supposed addition of some 20 stone gargoyles spaced along the roof edge beneath the embattlement of which only three remain (Pl. XIa).

But of these three demonic, fearsome guardians there are no indications of their having been appended to an existing structure. They seem integral, which, in my judgment, they are. There is nothing in the literature that tells us who were the artists, what architect designed their emplacement, or who was the ruler who gave the orders to make the physical change to the building. If integral, then the question arises as to the unlikely presence of an animal sculpture on a mosque. Mohammad had declared a proscription of animal or human representations in Islamic sacred buildings. My belief is that the sculptures were there from the beginning of construction, that they are Phoenician and that they were mostly destroyed by the Muslims since they objected to animal forms being exhibited on the building as part of its new incarnation as a mosque. The fearsome objects look like they could be part of a medieval cathedral which would suggest their having been added on after the Reconquista. But they could also be part of an earlier civilization's decor. How the symbolism would have reflected Phoenician society, I cannot say. But how much do we know of Phoenician symbolism?

The winged gargoyle in Pl. XIb has evidently a very strong structural and esthetic relationship to the projecting scupper above which, undoubtedly, serves to drain the roof. They are seemingly a unit which suggests that they are both original with the building. The scupper would look weak and inappropriate if it had no visible means of support of the gargoyle beneath it.

The symbolism of the bird sculpted on the interior face of the exterior wall on the northwest side is also not clear and should be investigated by archaeologists as to its possible Near East derivation (Pl. XIc). Curiously, it seems to be at home with the doves that now use the wall for roosting. It, too, is probably original with the building and not Islamic. Why would it be included in a mosque?

The new owners probably destroyed most of the gargoyle sculptures out of Islamic convictions but for some reason allowed a few to survive. To characterize this forbearance for the art of the previous eras as a sense of decency may be too generous. It is paralleled by the allowing to survive of the Elephant Gates of Fatehpur Sikri by the Moghul emperor Akbar in the 16th century in India. That tribute to Lakshmi, the great Hindu goddess and consort of Vishnu was expressed by the two stone elephants rising in tribute over the entry. To explain that anomaly, historians have strained all credulity by attributing its Islamic origin to the ecumenical breadth of vision of Akbar. Akbar, in spite of the good press he has been given by history, was a killer and a hater of pagans who somehow let the sculpture survive. But we all make mistakes.

Pl. XIa
Gargoyle

Pl. XIb
Exterior gargoyle

Pl. XIc Demonic bird gargoyle

12

Notes from the Underground

    Another consideration as to the supposed Islamic origin of the Mosque of Cordoba concerns the underground areas that exist beneath the main floor (Pl. XIIa). Mosques are not designed with basements. It is generally believed that the lower level of the Mosque of Cordoba incorporates the remains of earlier Roman streets that existed prior to the Muslim era. The southeast elevation has two or, perhaps, three levels, with no extant doorways. Could there have been doorways at the lower level that are now blocked off and that once opened into an underground level where goods from Phoenician ships were brought to be stored or where metals mined in Iberia could have been stored until loaded on ships for export?

    The full extent of the subterranean spaces is not known. The areas may be coextensive with the main areas of the mosque. What original purposes could they have served? We know very little about Phoenician architecture. Much that we do know is surmised from what we know of their Carthaginian followers who carried forward much of Phoenician culture.

    Evidence from Carthage suggests that their temples were combinations of temple, warehouse and audience hall. The lower levels may have been used for storage of heavy metals and as a source of ventilation for the main level which was used as storage for grain and other perishables. This was the method used extensively by Rome. Both Rome and Carthage made extensive use of large warehouse buildings to store materials for shipping or for prior amassing before distribution. Neither civilization had qualms about combining the sacred and the profane under one roof. Thus, a temple and warehouse combination was not unusual. While it is true that merchant countries then and now had to have extensive warehouse capabilities, there does not seem to be anything basically Roman in style about the mosque except, perhaps, for it seemingly classical columns in its interior. But the potential warehouse character of the building can be noted in the large hypostyle space and the typical generous areas that Roman and, probably, Carthaginian warehouses were accustomed to.

PL. XIIa
Lower level of mosque

13

From Tower to Minaret to Belfry

As we look at the mosque today, we may observe that one of its most prominent features is the minaret that looms high above the northwest perimeter wall (Pl. XIIIa). However, what we are looking at is actually a jacket of Renaissance design built in the 16th century to surround and conceal the ancient interior tower and to convert it to a bell tower to serve its new function as a cathedral belfry. A large portion of the original tower still exists and can be seen as one climbs the steps of the belfry tower. According to Torres Balbas, the concealed Islamic tower was a beautiful model for all subsequent minarets in Spain and later in the Maghrib, Marakesh, Rabat and Seville. He believes it to be the second tower of the mosque, replacing an earlier tower that was destroyed when the former northwest wall was moved further out to its present location. There is a masonry foundation that still exists in the prayer hall courtyard (sahn) that could have been the base for some other structure. It is said to have been the base for the former minaret.

Torres Balbas speaks of three metal balls that formerly existed at the top of the minaret as part of a finial representing perhaps apples—two golden and the middle one of silver—with two elegant series of six lily petals surrounding the middle ball. He describes a golden pomegranate at the very top having slightly less than one-half meter in height. Referring to Idrisi he believes that the entire minaret from grade to peak was covered on the exterior with beautiful painted decorations of gilt and inscriptions. The total effect of the minaret and its finial must have been very sumptuous and exciting. This would have been something well beyond the level of minaret building that the Muslims had achieved anywhere at that time.

The original exterior walls of the tower have been conserved to a height of 22 meters; the dividing wall in the center to 26 meters. Certain voussoirs built over some windows, Torres Balbas says, still have some paint on them. The tower rose in three tiers to a height of 73 meters and was crowned, if we accept a varied interpretation byIdrisi, not with three balls but with five metal balls shaped like apples—three of gold and two of silver—with leaves in the form of lilies (Dozy and deGoeje, pp. 13-14). One of the balls contained a large amount of oil which, Giminez estimates, held between ten and sixteen liters. Another author's description is of a pomegranate and two apples, both fruits popular in pre-Islamic Arabia. However, a finial crowned with natural symbolism is not typical of mosques which generally have a spike or a crescent. Since the upper part of the minaret is no longer extant, and the experts differ, we can only approximate what it looked like when first built.

The earliest mosques, according to Jonathon M. Bloom, American historian of Islamic art, had no minaret:

> While the minaret is the most prominent architectural feature of mosques, it is hardly known in early Islam. Fragmentary evidence indicates that the towers were not then standard features of Umayyad mosques. Two of the most important Umayyad mosques—in Damascus and Medina—are known to have had four corner towers, but the equally important Umayyad mosques in Jerusalem and Mecca had none. Therefore, the original function and meaning of these towers are specific to Damascus and Medina and do not indicate a general type. In the absence of any clear indications that these towers were built as places from which the call to prayer was given, I shall avoid using the term minaret. (Bloom, Five Fatimid Minarets in Upper Egypt, p. 164)

The call to prayer in early mosques was from within the perimeter wall or the court, or even from within the prayer hall. The first minarets appeared in Egypt and Syria and are said to have inspired their use across the Mediterranean to Spain to influence the Mosque of Cordoba:

> Generally antagonistic to the pretensions of the Abbasid caliphs of Baghdad, the Umayyads of Spain *appear* (my italics) to have accepted

the mosque tower by the middle of the 9th century, a period of strong Abbasid influence on all aspects of Andalusian culture and society. (Bloom, Five Fatimid Minarets in Upper Egypt, p. 165)

Bloom makes the interesting observation that whereas the Fatimids in Egypt avoided building mosque towers, not being interested in following the Baghdad lead in this matter, the Umayyads in Spain, who had, understandably, a strong antagonism to the Abbasid regime in Baghdad, apparently decided to emulate the Abassids or, perhaps, to distinguish themselves from the Fatimids who rejected the minaret. Dodds suggests that the paradoxical behavior of accepting the symbolism of the Abassids can be explained by the more pressing need to compete with Christian bell-towers. This is conceivable but Bloom makes a very clear statement that the overriding interest in minaret symbolism would have been a very strong deterrent to their having constructed the Cordoba minaret:

> Abd al-Rahman's son and successor, Hisham, may have added a staircase minaret to the mosque his father had built ... The tower attached to the mosque remained an Abassid innovation, however, and was found only in places clearly and closely allied with the tastes and policies of the capital. (Bloom, Minaret: Symbol of Islam, p. 95)

One must wonder if speculative hypothetical accepting or rejecting of the influence of Baghdad or Cairo on Spain by various scholars had anything to do with an unconscious attempt on their parts to avoid considering the prior existence of the minaret of the Mosque of Cordoba.

The minaret has a double stairway with 107 steps each of 94 centimeters clear width. If we count levels rather than risers that would be 108. It is a curious coincidence that 108 years equals, in Hindu lore, the existence of one Brahma. The life of kingship of an Indra lasts 71 eons; 28 eons equals one day and night of Brahma:

> The life and kingship of an Indra endure seventy-one eons, and when twenty-eight Indras have expired, one Day and Night of Brahma has elapsed. But the existence of one Brahma, measured in such Brahma Days and Nights, is only *one hundred and eight years (my italics).*

> Brahma follows Brahma; one sinks, the next arises; the endless series cannot be told. There is no end to the number of those Brahmas—to say nothing of the Indras. (Heinrich Zimmer, Myths and Symbols in Indian Art and Civilization, p. 6)

The ancient Vedic literature of India with its wealth of information on the archaic past of India presented in mythological form culminates in the final writings called the Upanishads, or the Vedanta, or end of the Vedas. In this philosophical compilation it is commonly agreed that the number of Upanishads is 108. (K. Antonova, A History of India, p. 55)

Another coincidence worth considering is that in Angkor, 108 is a special number:

> Phnom Bahkeng is a natural hill which the Khmers converted into a recessed pyramid. The central shrine is composed of five towers, and there are 104 smaller towers on the approaches to the summit.... the total number is 109.... the figure of 109 was important—the belief in a single polar axis around which there were 108 cosmic revolutions (1+108=109). The figure 108 is said to be a basic number of the large year.... Phnom Bakheng is the prime example of a diagram in time and space. (Christopher Pym, The Ancient Civilization of Angkor, p. 50)

And there are 108 gigantic stone figures in each of the five avenues of Angkor Thom, 54 on each side, a total of 540 statues. Each avenue of statues symbolizes the churning of the Milky Ocean, i.e. the Milky Way, our galaxy. It takes 72 years for the equinoxial sun to complete a precessional shift of one degree along the ecliptic. If we add one-half of 72 to itself we get 108. (de Santillana, Hamlet's Mill, 1969)

Marco Polo summed up his travels from Venice to China with some pertinent observations:

> Around the great white pagoda at Peking are 108 pillars for illumination. At Gautaru Buddha's birth 108 Brahmans were summoned to foretell his destiny ... Parashuram established (in Malabar) 108 places of worship (i.e. temples). Bharut has 108 holy places of pilgrimage and 108 Upanishads; the rules of the Chinese Triad Society assign 108

blows as the punishment for certain offences; according to Athenians the suitors of Penelope were 108. (Marco Polo, Memoirs, p. 347)

In Tibetan Buddhism their most popular boddhisatva and their patron saint has been Avalokiteshvara. He was their emblem, and remains so, of the supreme goal of mankind to dedicate oneself to salvation:

> Buddhist literature lists at least 108 forms for him, though in practise a select few are actually worshiped and portrayed. (Robert E. Fisher, The Art of Tibet, p. 44)

In a discussion of the donation of stupas in Tibet, or as they were known there, chortens, Robert E. Fisher tells us that there is an ancient tradition in Tibet that preceded the making of Buddha images that venerate sepulchral chortens. Here again the number 108 appears:

> Stupas continued to be donated after the completion of a temple, and active monasteries include many, of various sizes. Portable votive stupas, which could also include a relic, were commissioned and acquired as acts of merit. The best-known such donations was a group of 84,000 votive stupas offered by India's first great Buddhist king, Ashoka in the third century BC. The practice of dedicating auspicious numbers of stupas continued, as in the placing of 108 separate chortens, in even rows, in western Tibet—108 being the traditional number of delusions people have, according to various scriptures, and 84,000 the number of deities, the latter really standing for an infinitude. (Fisher, Art of Tibet, pp. 85-86)

Had Fischer dug deeper he might have found that the 108 chortens were not merely related to delusions as reported in scriptures but that they had a deeper astronomical significance. Could it be that Hindu and Asian scientific insights found their way to Iberia to influence the architecture of the Mosque of Cordoba?

The two stairways of the minaret had a dividing wall between them which separated the stairways so that someone using one stairway could not come into contact with a person on the other stairway until arriving at the top or bottom landings. The famous Pharos lighthouse of Alexandria, built in the 3rd century BC, which had three levels, also had a double staircase. Doris Behrens-Abousief identifies four minarets in Cairo with double, parallel stairways. She attributes this feature to a structural need to stiffen the points of contact between the core and the outer wall:

> Four minarets in Cairo have double, parallel stairways, arranged in such a way as to allow two persons to climb without encountering one another: the minarets of Quatbay and al-Ghuri art al-Azhar and the minarets of Azbak al-Yusufi and Khayrbak. Many minarets in Istanbul have such a double staircase. This feature is less pointless than it seems, since it strengthens the shaft by doubling points of contact between the core and the outer skin. (Behrens-Abousief, The Minarets of Cairo, p. 33)

Surely there are more economical and rational ways to strengthen a tower without resorting to the doubling of stairways. She offers no operational explanation for what seems to be a redundancy.

Perhaps it may be that two functions were designed for what were clearly distinctive purposes thus suggesting a walled separation. It may have been that the functions of lighthouse and watchtower were meant to be set off from its use as an astronomical observatory. A practical purpose for the dividing wall may have been to act as a firewall. With oil burning constantly above and oil being periodically brought up from below for lighthouse purposes, there may have been the need to keep the two stairs completely separate and fireproof so that fire could not spread from one side to the other, though what was exposed and flammable on the interior is not clear. The two stairs ascend in opposite directions, left and right, thus creating identical facades on the east and west. They meet at the same levels at grade and at the top.

The problem of finding a rational explanation for the double stairway ascending in opposite directions and mirroring each other may be that we are not casting a wide enough net. If we take our cue from Jerome Narby in his highly speculative book the Cosmic Serpent we can perhaps see in the stairways a symbol of the double helix which itself mirrors the cosmic serpent. Could it be that the source of all life, the double helix, is the real motive for the two stairs? How would they have known prior to the twentieth century of the double helix? Narby reasons that the double helix in the chromosome is a weak transmitter but that shamans, under the influence of drugs, can listen to and learn from the organic world at a microscopic level. Interesting but highly unlikely. Let me offer this possibility: the earlier civilization that actually produced the minaret recalled the symbols of knowledge that were known prior to the catastrophe. At this earlier time they may have been concerned about the symbolism of the spiral, as many ancient peoples were. This was certainly true of the Chinese. Here in the minaret the symbol may live again.

There were wooden frames embedded in the tower wall to act as ties or reinforcing bars holding the structure together at regular horizontal intervals as structural supports for the stairs, and embedded in the buttresses as vertical supports and bracing for the exterior walls (Fig. XIIIa). This seems to have been a typical construction method found in Islamic architecture in its earlier development. Or the method may have been in use in Spain for hundreds of years before. These frames should be thoroughly tested by carbon-14 dating. According to Idrisi, the wood comes from pine similar to what was used in the ceiling of the mosque and derives from the mountains that surround Tortosa. Being part of the structure they would be an excellent source for establishing the true date of construction of the tower.

The walls of the tower were made of large stones hollowed out in their interior, where required, to introduce wood beams. Felix Hernando Giminez describes wooden frames that were inserted in the stone wall for reinforcement (Fig. XIIIa):

> ... al embedido de dos or mas encadenados de madera en los muros de la torre para cosido de estos. (Hernando Giminez, <u>El Alminar de Abd Al-Rahman III en la Mezquita Mayor de Cordoba</u>, p. 43).
> (... *embedded are two or more wooden frames in the walls of the tower to support them*).

I took a sample in 1990 of one of the wood frames for carbon-14 dating which indicated a date range of 640 AD to 880 AD (Fig. Ia). The mid-point date is 710 AD, plus or minus 60 years. The mid-point date does not fall close to the accepted date of the construction of the minaret. But it does fall close to the beginning of the Islamic era in Spain. Evidently, either the tower was not of ancient Phoenician construction or it was repaired or rebuilt at a later date. It evidently was not a product of the tenth century AD.

The height of the minaret balcony from which the muezzin announced the five times daily call to prayer was 60 meters from the court below. It is not reasonable to accept the notion that it was designed for that purpose. At that height it would have been very inefficient as a call to prayer since the human voice could hardly carry down to the ground and out far enough to the town. A minaret must have a practical minimum and maximum height for the voice of the muezzin to carry to the streets below. Nor is the site of this congregational mosque at the Guadalquivir's edge convenient for calling to prayer or for that matter for assembling the faithful. A central location in the midst of the community would have been more suitable. To the southeast is only the prayer hall and the river; to the southwest is the palace of the Alcazar; to the northwest was the Jewish quarter; and to the northeast and northwest was the mass of the Muslim population. Since the minaret was not in the midst of the Islamic population, reaching them by voice to the outer limits of their quarters would have been difficult if not impossible. The balcony, which orients 360 degrees, would have been of little value in two directions and of limited value in the other two.

But as an ancient watchtower/lighthouse from which one could scan for boats coming up the Gaudalquivir River or from which one could be on the lookout for enemy armies approaching the city by land, it would have served critical needs. Relays of signals could have been forwarded from the tower to the meeting hall, then on to the city's perimeter wall defenses and beyond to a series of signal towers within relay reach of each other. Signal lighthouses were used in the Middle East to relay messages as far away as from one country to another. The metal balls at the finial of this tower could have been used to hold oil as fuel for the fire of the signal light. The term amanar or manara means the same as ma'dhana in Arabic or minaret but also means lighthouse or watchtower:

> ... the term manar or manara, which is used in medieval documents and inscriptions to mean the same as ma'dhana. It means a place from which light is supplied and is therefore used to designate a lighthouse or watchtower. (Behrens-Abousief, pp. 11-12)

She points out the historical distinction between a tower and a minaret and that the tower is the true origin of the minaret. It functions well as a watchtower/signal tower and astronomical observatory but its great height would have made it inefficient as a call to prayer. As Bloom has indicated as well, Behrens-Abousief offers several examples of towers that served as watchtowers and also as minarets, or were later turned into minarets:

> Essentially a tower, it is no wonder that in many Islamic countries the early minaret borrowed from pre-Islamic tower architecture. Early minarets in Iran, Central Asia and North Africa were similar to previously existing watchtowers: the tower of Qasr al-Hayr al-Sharqi in Jordan could have been a watchtower or a minaret, or perhaps both; and the towers used by the Coptic monks for their retreats in the desert *were later turned into minarets* (my italics*)*. It is probable that such origins never entirely disappeared. Outside urban centers minarets built as such continued to be used as watchtowers as well, as has been suggested, for instance in the case of the Upper Egyptian Fatimid minarets. The great minaret of the Omayyad mosque at Damascus is reported by Qalqashandi to have been a link in a chain of towers connecting Mesopotamia, Syria and Egypt with *a system of fire signals to give the alarm* (my italics) in case of a Mongol attack. The mosque said to have been erected by Ibn Tulun on the site of a pre-Islamic lighthouse on the Muqattam hill likewise had a minaret equipped with a light to guide travelers in the night. (Behrens-Abousief, p. 12)

The Cordoba tower is believed to have been built as part of the Stage III expansion of the mosque by Abd-ar Rahman III in 951 AD. It allegedly replaced an earlier minaret built by Hisham I in Phase I in 793 AD. As part of Phase III of construction by Abd-ar Rahman III, he is said to have strengthened the northwest wall of the prayer hall by doubling each column and erecting a second wall in order to repair and strengthen the original wall which was, perhaps, weakened by an earthquake. He is also credited with having moved the perimeter court wall some 20 meters north to its present location. The new minaret is said to have been built then into the new perimeter wall. At that time, he allegedly tore down the no longer needed original minaret. Foundations for this earlier minaret were claimed to have been uncovered in 1934 according to Levy-Provencal. Or it may be that an earthquake in 880 AD caused the destruction of the earlier minaret thus necessitating a new one:

> Abd al-Rahman III, besides reconstructing the front of the mosque, rebuilt (945-46) Hisham's minaret, which was only 40 cubits high, and had been overthrown in the earthquake of 880. The new one was a square tower, some say 72 and some say over 100 cubits in height, ascended by a double staircase. It was embellished by mosaics, and encircled by a double tier of arches. At the top was a kiosk crowned by three balls of gold and silver between two flowers, the whole surmounted by a golden pomegranate. (Rivoira, <u>Moslem Architecture</u>, p. 364)

But still another scholar, Gomez, asserts that in Ibn Idhari's description of the earthquake damage, as reported by Bayan, he makes no mention of any destruction of the first minaret. Lambert notes that there is no text that speaks of an enlargement of the sahn (prayer hall) to the north and we do not actually know when this occurred. The old minaret was allegedly built by Hisham I at the end of the 8th century. The new one must have been built, he reasons, by Abd ar-Rahman III in 945-946, and that it must have been erected to overcome the first minaret's isolation when the addition to the north was made. Considering all the speculation and disagreement, can we be sure there ever was a first minaret or tower? Was the perimeter wall ever actually moved? The absence of construction joints, previously mentioned, does not support that contention.

A question must be raised again concerning construction time. It is said to have taken three months to build the new tower. It was acclaimed as the tallest minaret in the world at that time. Three months of construction hardly seems adequate. But if it were for the rehabilitation of an existing structure, it could have been accomplished. The same skepticism should prevail regarding al-Razi's report that Phase I of the mosque was built in five months. Considering the forest of stone columns, their elaborate arched connectors, the gabled roof sections above the aisles, the necessary foundations and undefined basement area, it would have taken a much longer time. This realization prompted later commentators to revise their estimates. Probably, the extent of Islamic construction consisted of removing rubble from the existing but damaged building, columns were replaced where required, pagan statuary and epigraphy were removed and Islamic epigraphy was put in place.

Pl. XIIIa Renaissance cover over tower

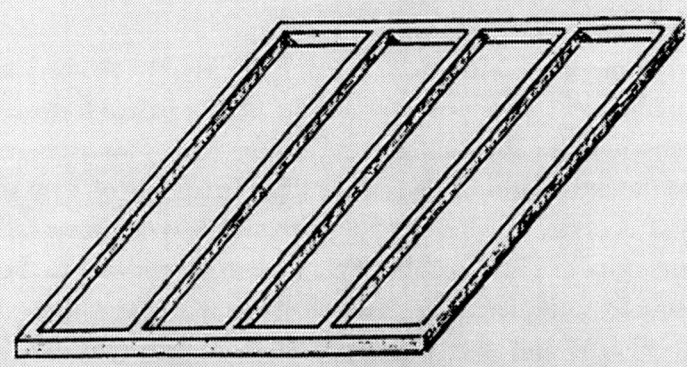

Mezquita Mayor de Cordaba, alminar de 'Abd al-Raḥmān III: detalle de uno de los encadenados de madera

**Fig. XIIIa
Wood frame reenforcing
of tower**

14

The Palace City of Madina Azahara

The relation of the Mosque of Cordoba to Madina Azahara is that of a prime building of a river port city and its nearby palace fortress city. The fortress city is about three miles west of Cordoba. This arrangement was similar to the relationship between the Phoenician city of Tyre and its fortress city, Paleotyre, or what the Egyptian and Assyrian texts called Ushu. The fortress city of Ushu enabled Tyre to control territory to the south. It was eventually conquered by Nebuchadnezzar. (Marie Eugenia Aubet, The Phoenicians and the West, pp. 30-31). Paleotyre was known as "ancient Tyre" and was situated on the mainland. This model of urban planning may have inspired the Cordoban relation of port city and fortress city.

It is not likely that Madina Azahara was built originally either by the Romans or by Islam though they both, undoubtedly, made good use of it. Its central axis is approximately 24 degrees east of north—an orientation for settlements not characteristic of the Romans who strongly preferred the cardinal directions. Its rich and beautiful architectural interior forms are in many ways similar to the forms used in the Mosque of Cordoba indicating that Madina Azahara also owed no cultural affinity to Rome or Islam. There are basically too many features that are independent of the traditions of both cultures.

As demonstrated above, the Mosque of Cordoba, when judged from a functional point of view, worked poorly as a mosque. Its form, its minaret, its asymmetry, its lack of orientation to Mecca, its superfluous basement, its unprecedented mihrab room, its incongruous gargoyles—all point to some original function other than as a mosque. Like the mosque, the palace city of Madina Azahara also exhibits, as a Muslim complex, a confusion of specific functional interrelationships and other anomalies. Instead of being designed as a palace-city for the Umayyads of Spain, it may actually have been originally the main Phoenician fortress and palatine city for Andalusia—their Versailles.

The sculpted arabesque wall plaques have symmetrical, self-contained design patterns rather than infinitely expanding patterns which would be typical of Islamic design (Pl. XVa). Above the entrance gate at the south wall enclosure is said to have existed a statue of Venus which, on the contrary, the local people identified with a favorite of the caliph. It is unlikely that the Muslims would have introduced a three-dimensional realistic sculpture in such a prominent location. It is more likely that it was a Phoenician statue of Astarte who later became identified with Venus, the goddess of love, and then later became an Islamic symbol on the Azahara wall. Marianne Barrucand and Achim Bednorz write:

> According to the written sources, Abd ar-Rahman III named his new creation after his favorite wife, a certain Zahra. A statue of this favorite is said—according to al-Maqqari, an Arab historian of the 16th/17th century—to have adorned the main gate of the city, and to have remained intact until it was destroyed by the Almahadic Caliph Ya'qub al-Mansur. Unfortunately, al-Maqqari's sources are not always reliable, and a statue of the loved one above the city gate is *inherently improbable* (my italics). Nothing comparable is known from any part of the Western Islamic world, and while statues above palace entrances are known from the Islamic Near East in the 8th century, women were never among those thus depicted. (Barrucand and Bednorz, Moorish Architecture in Andalusia, p. 61)

However, the mosque in Madina Azahara may be an original mosque (Fig. 14b, no. 83). Its peripheral location east of the South Terrace and at a lower level, remote from the palace and the mass of the people, suggests that it was the last best site available. The palace living quarters to the northwest are some 300 meters away from the mosque and about 38 meters higher up on the slope, a location which would have been very inconvenient for the royalty in their attendance at the mosque. Instead of being, as it is alleged, the first building to have been built at Azahara in 941, it may have been the last. It faces Mecca because it was probably built by the Muslims to fulfill the basic orientation requirement of a mosque. It superficially resembles the Mosque of Cordoba, though it is much smaller, probably because it was patterned after that existing building. This would account for the fact that, while the Cordoba Mosque does not face Mecca, the Azahara Mosque apparently does.

On the other hand, the Azahara mosque may have been originally a pre-existing Phoenician temple, reworked and used as a mosque. If that were the case, why is it apparently facing Mecca? The explanation may be that the Azahara mosque and the Kaaba at Mecca had a relationship that antedated the Islamic era and this was reflected in the orientation of the Azahara mosque to Mecca. It would account for the confusion concerning the exact date it was built and how long it took to build. Inscriptions on the mosque say that it took four years to build, but the historian al-Maqqari (d. 1631-2) says it took only 48 days to build.

Whereas the Azahara mosque was described by al-Maqqari as having been built with amazing speed, the whole palace city, he says, took forty years to build. Why the desperate pace for the construction of the mosque and the apparently relaxed pace for the city as a whole? After all, the somewhat apocryphal Azahira palace city built about three miles east of Cordoba, they say, by al-Mansur, the minister of the the new caliph Hisham II after Al-Hakim's death, is said to have taken only two years to build. Based on al-Maqqari's historian of choice, Ibn Hayyan (d. 1106-7), he catalogued how during construction, beginning in 936-937, Azahara made use of 400 columns, 15,000 door leafs, and 10,000 workmen and slaves. Yet, the detailed account does not include an account of excavation. The explanation may be that he is describing rework, not original construction.

It is interesting to note that the water supply to Azahara was said to be new construction; that it continued on beyond Azahara to supply Cordoba and the Great Mosque. If this were true, why haven't scholars raised the question: what did Cordoba and its Great Mosque do for water before Azahara was built? It is more likely that the port of Cordoba, its temple/

warehouse and its palace-city were all built at the same time by the Phoenicians, and that a water system was built to serve all three at once. The four-part upper pools and gardens on the South Terrace of Azahara were part of the varied and intricate water supply system (Fig. XIVb, no. 76). That four-part theme is the same theme used at the gardens of the Court of the Lions in the Alhambra and the gardens of the Taj Mahal, a design that derives from earlier Persian and Indian garden design. The water systems of Azahara and the Alhambra have common features suggesting a common origin. Both are supplied by water courses, fountains and cisterns. In addition, both complexes have rooms surrounding interior courts; both are encircled by walled fortifications; both are on a height commanding a valley; and both have exterior walls that are formidable and plain while their interiors are light and delightful.

On ceremonial occasions there may have been a processional movement from Azahara to the Mosque of Cordoba (then the Temple of Melqarth). Moving first through Azahara's magnificent archways to the northeast (Pl. XIVa), proceeding east three and a half miles to the port city of Cordoba, turning south down the main avenue to the entry at the mosque wall alongside the observation tower (later the minaret), across the sahn (court), down the wide central nave to the inner sacred area (later to become the maqsura).

The focal point of Azahara is the Salon Rico (Rich Hall) whose fabulous decorative and sculptural forms of columns and arches are a delight to the eye. The light-hearted and charming horseshoe arches with alternating voussoirs and the refreshing mixture of blue and pink columns on the exterior tell us that the architects were reflecting optimistic and joyful aspirations of the society that sponsored the projects. It may have been the main reception hall for the Phoenicians. We can only guess, which is what authors have always been doing regarding medieval Islamic history, but with greater claim to authority. Antonio Vallejo Triano, expert at the Conjunto Arqueológico de Medina-Zahara in Cordoba, makes an attempt at explaining the Salon Rico which merits a close examination:

> This building, also presently known as the Salon Rico (Rich Hall) because of the extravagant decoration of the walls, was ordered constructed by Abd al-Rahman III between 953/4 and 956/7 (A.H. 342-45), as attested by plentiful epigraphical evidence. Facing the Dar al-jund, the building was solely devoted to audiences. Its space is unified in concept: Two series of horseshoe arches of magnificent caliphal proportions separate three principal aisles, of which the central arch is a true mihrab, as is recorded in written sources." (Triano, *"Madinat al-Zahra: The Triumph of the Islamic State"*, p. 33)

Triano accepts without question the epigraphical evidence attesting to Abd al-Rahman having ordered the construction of the Salon Rico. He fails to acknowledge that script on the face of the building can be readily applied long after a building is built. This was common practice in Andalusia by the Muslims and, indeed, in many other countries of the world. He may be right that the space was devoted to audiences but the question is: which audiences originally? He describes the horseshoe arches as being of "magnificent caliphal proportions". Muslim architecture owes a great deal to the adaptation of and the borrowing of forms. The horseshoe arch clearly preceded the advent of Islam. He refers to the central arch as a "true mihrab". But a mihrab is a niche in the wall whose shape can vary considerably. That it was described "in written sources" does not make it Muslim especially since these sources are of a later date.

PL. XIVa
Eastern Arcade
Medina Azahara

15

The Alhambra

The control of the Cadiz—Cordoba axis that extended along the Guadalquivir River guaranteed that the main hinterland areas of Tartessos were secure for Phoenician trade. Cadiz dominated the commercial relations with the Tartessian Rio Tinto silver mines area around Huelva, near Cadiz. Cordoba and its palatine military encampment Madina Azahara controlled the river valley and its agricultural and mineral products. What then was the role of the Alhambra? Originally, it may have been a fortified Phoenician government center designed to control the hinterland area near the Mediterranean coast where the Phoenician settlements of Toscanos, Chorreras and Almuneçar were located and afford protection to these colonies.

There existed what Aubet calls, an "authentic Phoenician coast" between Gibraltar and Alicante. The Mediterranean coastal settlements thrived in a state of peaceful coexistence with their Tartessian indigenous neighbors whose settlements preceded those of the Phoenicians. It was not the peoples on the coast that required military control but peoples in the hinterland. It was remarkable that there was apparently no imperial domination involved with the Tartessians supplying the raw materials and the labor while the Phoenicians supplied the trade. The eighth century BC settlements of both peoples existed side by side.

> ... a commercial enterprise such as that of the Phoenicians could have established prolonged trade relationships only with societies that were capable of guaranteeing the flow of surplus goods and procuring native labor in the ports, mines and fields—and all this in a state of stability, peace, and continuity of interchanges. (Maria Eugenia Aubet Semmler,

"Phoenician Trade in the West: Balance and Perspectives", in *The Phoenicians in Spain*, edited by M. Bierling, p. 102)

Like many Phoenician settlements, the Alhambra was located on a height for security with the help of an encircling red sandstone wall from which the name "alhambra" or red fort, in Arabic, was later derived. There are certain problems with the current explanation of the Alhambra originating as an Islamic palace-city of the thirteenth to fifteenth centuries, supposedly mainly a product of the Nasrid dynasty which ruled Granada from 1237 to 1492. Granada was the last gasp of power of Islam in Spain. Oleg Grabar, a leading historian of Islamic art, refers to the regime as "moribund". Would the Muslims in decline have built an ambitious and expensive project in that period? It is more reasonable to expect that they would have retrenched and hunkered down in anticipation of the final onslaught by the Reconquista. But if it were primarily a matter of reworking what was already there, they could have made use of the many craftsmen and artists who had flocked to the area as the rest of Spain succumbed to the Christian wave of conquest.

As at the Mosque of Cordoba and Madina Azahara the question of fitness to function in the Alhambra must be examined. It is not known why the rooms were arranged the way they were and how they functioned. Names attributed to the rooms like the Hall of the Sisters are only fanciful later Spanish titles based on legend. Grabar, in confronting this problem, concludes that they must have been designed in a random, non-functional fashion:

> It may be, perhaps, that the medieval Islamic world never developed any specificity of meaning in their palace architecture and that all these buildings, whatever the reasons for their construction, were simply considered as settings for whatever life happened from time to time to take place in them. Even when one can propose a concrete explanation for the forms and immediate connotations of a princely monument, the monument itself did not reflect precise specifications of ceremonial or practical use, being intended merely as an elaborate shell for man to use as he saw fit. (Grabar, p. 156)

Because there is little evidence based on documents and chronicles concerning the origin of the Alhambra, making it difficult to establish the purposes for the parts of the complex, he falls back on an improbable theory of architectural design. But, to my knowledge, there are few precedents, if any, in the history of architecture that demonstrate random design of key rooms and buildings. Designing an all—purpose space is one thing but a space without any purpose, a shell for any activity, is highly unlikely. Architecture, universally, responds in some purposeful manner to clients' needs. The needs may be symbolic or cultural, but needs, nonetheless.

In what has been referred to as the "Bargebuhr hypothesis", there is strong evidence of an earlier origin. Frederick P. Bargebuhr, a German scholar who died in 1965, points out that in a famous poem, Ibn Gabirol (d. 1052), the great Spanish Jewish poet, describes a palace court so vividly that in Bargebuhr's view it could only have been the Alhambra's Court of the Lions:

> In the palace high above all its surroundings
>   and built of precious stones;
> Built to rise from a firm foundation,
>   its walls fortified with towers.
> And the leveled plateau surrounds it;
>   roses adorn all the courtyards.
> The buildings are built and decorated
>   with openwork; intaglios and filigrees.
> Paved with marble slabs and alabaster—
>   I cannot count its many gates.
> And the doors are like those of the ivory mansions
>   reddened by palatial sandalwoods.
> And the windows, transparent above them
>   are skylights where dwell the heavenly planets,
> The dome is like the Palanquin of Solomon,
>   hanging above the rooms' splendours,

> That rotates in its circumference, shining like
> > bedellium and sapphire and pearls....
> And there is a full sea, like unto Solomon's Seas,
> > though not on oxen it stands,
> But there are lions, in phalanx by its rim,
> > roaring for prey—these whelps
> Whose bellies are wellsprings that spout forth
> > through their mouths floods like streams.
> And there are hinds embedded in the channels,
> > hollowed out as water spouts
> To douse the plants in the beds,
> And upon the lawns to shed clear waters ...
> And also to water the myrtle garden;
> > they sprinkle the tree tops like clouds.
> (Bargebuhr, *"The Alhambra Palace of the Eleventh Century"*, pp. 192-258)

Bargebuhr feels so strongly about the value of the evidence of the poem as an indication of the prior 11th century existence of the Alhambra and its lion fount that he can only comprehend denial as resulting from ignorance or political bias:

> ... we do not doubt that the rest of the castle, including the Fount of the Lions, as described by Ibn Gabirol, existed during his time. Such a doubt could spring only from unfamiliarity with this type of panegyric poetry with its accepted documentary value, or from a prejudice which has its origin in political fears and interests, and which will imperil true historical investigations, even after 900 years.(Bargebuhr, The Alhambra, p. 192)

It is reasonable to wonder in historical circumstances like this, where there may have been modification of an existing building rather than a new one built, why we do not have the testimony of witnesses to its earlier existence? In this case we have besides Gabirol's poem, a reference to an earlier

Jewish construction during the Zirid dynasty that preceded the Nasrids noted in the "Memoirs" of Abdallah b. Buluggin (1064-1090), the last Zirid king of Granada. My translation from the French:

> However, the gulf between the Jew and the population continued to widen and the friction increased. The Jew, fearing the populace, dismantled his residence to reside in the Alcazaba, just at the moment when his hopes were about to be realized. That earned him the disapproval of the people, in spite of his efforts in the construction of the Alhambra fortress, where he had planned to relocate with his family when Ibn Sumadih penetrated Granada, just at the time when the situation was becoming stable …

Allusion here is being made to palace construction by the powerful Jewish vizier Samuel Nagrallah and his son Jusuf. On the southwest slope of the Alhambra hill was the Jewish quarter connected to the fortress by the Vermillion towers and gate. The XIth century Alhambra was probably built on the foundations and ample remains of the Phoenician Alhambra to protect the large Jewish population of Granada who were prosperous and influential.

It is interesting that one scholar, Dario Cabanelas Rodriguez, does not rule out the possibility of an earlier castle existing in Roman times while agreeing that there is abundant evidence for a Jewish castle erected in the eleventh century:

> It is not possible to say whether buildings existed on the site of the present Alhambra during the time of the Romans and the Visigoths. (Cabanelas Rodriguez, p.133)

The next question he could have asked was whether there may have been an even earlier palace, one whose walls and foundations still survive? We know so little of Phoenician history in Andalusia that, at this point, we can only conjecture. But the absence of affirmative evidence of a Phoenician presence in Granada should not rule out its having been there and that the Phoenician palace city is still basically intact. The question is: Which of the three possible castles do we basically see today? Could it be that the existing elegant finishes and Koranic inscriptions are only repairs and cosmetic refinements of Castle 3 (Nasrid), of Castles 2 (Zirid), and of Castle 1 (Phoenician)?

We have in the Alhambra similar disturbing anomalies that we discussed regarding the Mosque of Cordoba. The apparently two small extant Alhambra mosques do not face Mecca. Nor do they both face in the same direction. This throws doubt on the assertion that they were originally intended to be mosques. And the supposed use of the Cuarto Dorado's south wall as the location for a throne for the king to receive visitors is almost too ridiculous to comment on. It is obviously too cramped a space and would have been beset by pedestrian traffic. There is the question, too, about the lack of solid information concerning the location of a large mosque ample enough to serve the congregation in the vicinity of the palace as well as the absence of a mosque in the fortified western part called the Alcazaba. All of these questions and more diminish the credibility of the concept of a supposed Islamic attribution of the palace.

My imaginative reconstruction drawing suggests how the Alhambra may have originally been designed as a Phoenician administrative and military center comparable to Madina Azahara (Fig. XVa). A characteristic feature of ancient eastern Mediterranean cities from the time of the Bronze Age has been the provision for ceremonies that traverse the area by means of a "processional way". This is reminiscent of the route through the Ishtar Gate in Babylon of the 6th century BC and the procession from Athens to its Acropolis in the 5th century BC. In a similar manner, to Granada from the plain below, up the slopes of the hill, processional enfilades may have made their way up to the encircling wall, through the Vermilion Towers, ascended the walk up to the Gate of Law, through the Wine Gate, on to a plaza (where at a later time the Renaissance Palace of the sixteenth century was built), through the Court of the Myrtles and on to the Hall of the Ambassadors. The goal of the procession may have been the Phoenician temple, now called the Hall of the Ambassadors, with nine surrounding chapels, each perhaps devoted to a separate Phoenician deity. This would have been the most important room in the complex.

Henri and Ann Stierlin believe that the Alhambra was modeled after the Palace of Solomon, that the Court of the Myrtles and the Court of the Lions are patterned after the courts in the Palace of Solomon, and the original 11th century ceiling in the Throne Room or Hall of the Ambassadors was an intricate and moving cosmological diagram, a vaulted planetarium patterned after Solomons baldachin over the throne of Solomon's Palace:

> À l'Alhambra, chez des Arabs passés maîtres dans la construction des astrolabes, des spheres armillaires et autres instruments d'observation du ciel, on peut donc aisément postuler l'existence d'un tel mécanism emblematique et de consultation horoscopique, réservé à l'usage exclusif du sultan, auquel il confère un pouvoir supérieur. Les textes, les inscriptions at même les vestiges in situ conforte cette conclusion: en effet, le plafond de marqueterie analysé par, Dario Cabanelas avec ses représentations stellaires, ne serait que la survivance figée d'un vaste planetarium en forme de couronne qui devait orner la salle du trône de l'Alhambra, avant que ne s'écroule la coupole à stalactites que le dôme en bois est venu remplacer dès le 15ième siècle. (H. and A. Stierlin, *"Jardins et bâtiments cosmiques sous les Nasrides"*, p.78) *(In the Alhambra, typical of the ability of the Arabs to be past masters in devising astrolabes, models of the celestial spheres ... and other instruments of observation of the sky, one can therefore readily postulate the existence of such a symbolic mechanism with horoscopic insights, reserved for the use of the sultan, which conferred on him a superior power. The texts, the inscriptions and even the vestiges that remain in place support this conclusion: in effect, the wood marquetry surface analyzed by Dario Cabanelas with its stellar representations, could only be the figurative survival of a vast planetarium in the form of a crown which would embellish the throne room of the Alhambra, before the collapse of the stalactite cupola which replaced the wood dome in the 15th century.)*

Therefore, he accepts the view that the symbolism of the Alhambra dates to the 10th century BC. The references to Solomon's Temple may be true. This may be so, not because it was an Islamic recall of a Phoenician/Jewish symbolism of more than a thousand years earlier, but because the Hall of the Ambassadors was originally devised by the Phoenicians as a combination seat of royalty, center of religion and astronomical planetarium and observatory. The Court of the Lions and its surrounding buildings and rooms probably housed the top Phoenician administrators in Andalusia and then served a similar purpose with new rulers when the Zirid and Nasrid dynasties were later in power.

It is, likewise, more reasonable to assume that the famous Lion's Fountain, the focal point of the Court of the Lions, was Phoenician rather than Islamic. This would explain the perplexing anomaly of naturalistic sculpture in an Islamic building. Its style is more appropriate to Phoenician art than to Islamic art. Bargebuhr has pointed out that the twelve lions supporting the overflowing basin is an interpretation of the "brazen sea", the bronze fountain in front of Solomon's Temple in Jerusalem, similarly had an overflowing basin, but it was supported by twelve oxen rather than lions.

The lions have a striking resemblance to what has been identified as a Scythian gold ornamental object by the Metropolitan Museum of Art. It was part of their exhibition on Scythian art which they described:

> This elaborate object, photographed on a mirror, is one of a pair and its function is unknown. It somewhat resembles Iranian works in style and in the use of inlay, and may have been made on the western borders of the Achaemenid empire. It was one of two pieces withdrawn from the exhibition because of their fragility.... (The Land of the Scythians, Ancient Treasures from the Museums of the U.S.S.R., 3000 B.C.-100 B.C., The Metropolitan Museum of Art and the Los Angeles County Museum of Art)

The very close resemblance can be discerned in the shape of the eye sockets, the shape of the fierce mouth with its fangs and squared teeth, the bridge of the nose, the whiskers and the shape of the ears. That so many feline characteristics could be similar must lead one to wonder if their resemblance is more than accidental. The provenance of both the lions of the fount and the Scythian lions is likely to be the same and that could be by way of the Near East. It is known that the Scythians had penetrated into Europe by, at the latest, the 6th century BC and had transmitted much of their art heritage to the Celts whose culture prevailed from Hungary to Spain. It supports my contention that the Scythian source of the lions was transmitted by the Phoenicians. The original Alhambra was Phoenician and from a period of time when the Scythians were at the height of power. The figurative style of the sculpture would not normally have been purposefully chosen by an Islamic client and designer.

Robert Irwin is a British historian who has written extensively on Arab and Muslim history and culture. Irwin is correct in his view that the fountain could not have been some afterthought that was plunked into the court after the court was designed and built. He points out that the size of the lion fountain was fixed by drawing arcs from the corners of the patio to the edges of the doorways of the two domed rooms on the north and the south—the Hall of the Two Sisters and the Hall of the Abencerrages—with the edges of the fountain fitting precisely within the intersection of those arcs. He concludes:

> The proportions of the fountain in the Court of the Lions and their harmonious relation to the rest of the courtyard indicate that the fountain was not plundered from some earlier building but was indeed sculpted as the centerpiece for this particular layout. (Irwin, p. 116)

That the Court of the Myrtles and the Court of the Lions were built as a unified whole was accurately demonstrated by the use of generating lines and geometric relationships by Henri and Ann Stierlin (H. and A. Stierlin, The Alhambra). They proved that the palace was conceived as a unit and did not grow essentially by accretion. Therefore, Irwin's explanation of the growth of the Alhambra from the ninth century western spur of the Qasaba to the time of the Zirids and the Nasrids is not tenable. It was designed all at once. A possible grand reception hall could have existed earlier on the east side of a plaza as I indicated in my imaginative reconstruction (Fig. XVa).

Robert Irwin, Arabist and novelist, in his interesting discussion in 2004 of the Alhambra in The Alhambra takes up the issue of the role of proportions in the design of the Court of the Lions. He refers to the work of the architectural historian George Marçais and Fernández-Puertas, the leading

Spanish expert on the Alhambra, who both recognized the use of proportion and ratios in the design of the Court of the Lions:

> As Fernández-Puertas notes, this was the only 'palace' to be designed by a single architect and built as a single unit within a single reign (that of Muhammad V). His exposition of the proportions of the court of the lions supersedes the earlier and more loosely argued theory propounded by the architectural historian Georges Marçais in the 1950s that the spacing of the arches and columns in the Court of the Lions was dictated by the golden mean, a proportional relation in which the ratio of width to length is the same as that of length to the sum of width and length. *It is not clear that Muslim builders and designers ever made use of proportional relationships based on the golden mean* (my italics). (Irwin, The Alhambra, pp. 110-111)

Both Fernández-Puertas and Gerges Marçais are aware of the mathematical bases for the design of the Court of the Lions though they disagree as to how exactly it was applied. But Marçais makes the off-hand remark that we don't know of any commitment by Muslim builders to the golden mean. He might have added: nor is there solid evidence of their having been guided by mathematical proportions. The sense of ratio and proportion is attributed to the Muslims as hindsight since we "know" that they built the Alhambra. Irwin sympathizes with Fernández-Puertas' strained insights into Muslim historical design practice but excuses it:

> Fernández-Puertas has had to work with the faintest of indications, and there is not much evidence for any aspect of the history of this palace. Those who have not worked as professional historians on the medieval past can have no idea of how little of that past survives, how many sources from which one might have reconstructed that past have *vanished irretrievably*"(my italics*). (*Irwin, The Alhambra, *p. 117)*

The evidence is scarce but it may be because it was never there rather than its having "vanished". He could have questioned the Muslim provenance of the palace when he admitted:

> Although numerous medieval Arab treatises on geometry have survived, there are no discussions of the application of geometry to esthetic design ... (Irwin, p.118)

Irwin condescendingly allows that Grabar's limited appreciation of Bargebuhr's hypothesis is stimulating so he devotes a few pages to oppose any suggestion that there may have been prior Jewish or Persian references in the palace. He prefers the solid tome of Fernandez-Puertas with its detailed investigation. But Irwin, Grabar, Bargebuhr, Marçais, and Fernández-Puertas all missed the opportunity to examine a critical possibility: the Alhambra was older than the Muslim era. The suggestion by Bargebuhr that the Zirid vizier Samuel Naghralla, in the 1050s, was seeking to recreate the vanished grandeur of the Madina Azahara, links the two complexes historically and makes the theory of their common ancestry more acceptable. But what was their common ancestry?

The Phoenicians were quite capable esthetically and technologically of producing the Alhambra. Many centuries elapsed giving them the time and experience to develop their high level of civilization including their architecture. The influence of the Tartessians may have enriched their creativity even further. Architecture appeared in the Mediterranean long before 1200 BC when it touched down in the form of some settlements in Spain. Phoenician power had 500 years to mature in Andalusia until it reached its height in the 7th century BC. By the sixth century BC Phoenician rule was replaced by the Carthaginians. There is a certain lightness and grace in Phoenician esthetics displayed in the various artifacts that have been discovered which suggests a society that is relatively humanistic, joyous and comfortable. In contrast to the grim cast that has been placed on the later Carthaginian society due to its sacrifice of children, this earlier society was apparently different and more humanistic. Strangely enough, the best evidence of the architecture of the Phoenicians is depicted on the Nineveh palace wall slabs made during the reign of Sennacherib (705-681 BC) and on the Balawat doors made during the reign of Shalmaneser III (858-824 BC) which show Phoenician cities like Tyre being conquered or subservient to Assyria or Assyrians standing on the shores ready to receive merchandise. Characteristics of the architecture, that can also be noted in the Mosque of Cordoba, include the imposing fortified presence, the grand use of arcuation, the placement of piers at regular intervals, the crenellations on top of the walls, and the mastery of masonry construction. The elegance of the architecture does not seem to have been true of their inheritors, the Carthaginians, whose imperial ambitions and militaristic society were reflected in more somber art forms.

What is really needed to get to the heart of the Alhambra's origin is more intensive archaeological work on Phoenicia. The total contemporary research and scholarly interest in Phoenicia receives only a fraction of the effort and money dedicated to investigating ancient Greece, Rome and Egypt. Part of the problem is that modern cities sit on the sites of ancient Phoenician cities and one can understand the reluctance of people living there today to upset these sites.

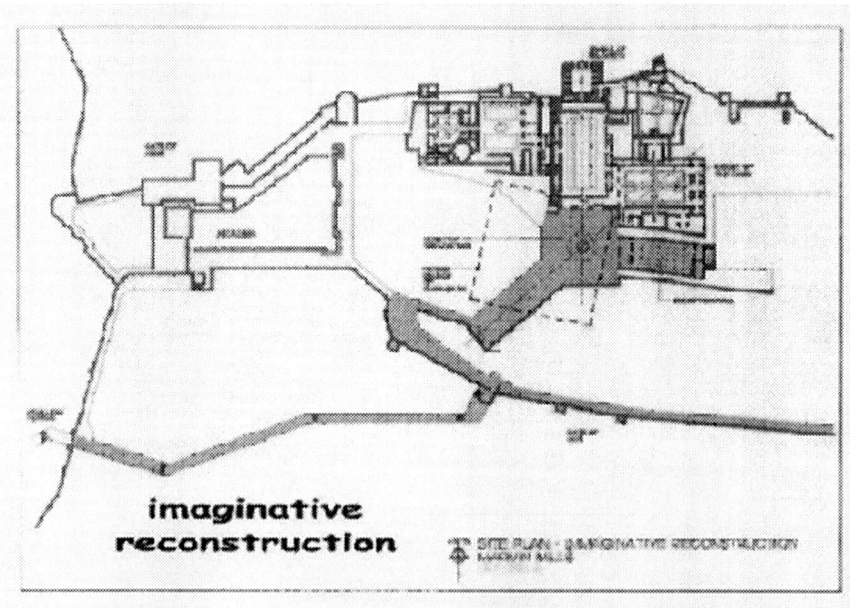

Fig. XVa
Site plan of the Alhambra

16

A New Paradigm

What I like to think of as a unified field theory of the origins of the Mosque of Cordoba, Madina Azahara and the Alhambra responds favorably to many of the problems raised by the standard paradigm which assumes their Islamic origins. This new overview accounts for the alleged sudden or mature appearance of supposed bold Islamic forms such as the horseshoe arch, the double arch, the monumental minaret and the chambered mihrab in the Mosque of Cordoba; it offers an explanation for the undefined function of spaces within the Alhambra and Madina Azahara complexes; it provides insights into the astronomical alignments, building orientations and site locations; and it suggests an alternative role for the buildings as part of Phoenician history. The next investigative step, using this new framework of interpretation, should be to continue to date these buildings scientifically by means of Carbon-14, thermoluminescence analysis and other archaeometric means of scientific dating of multiple samples to determine at least which centuries we are talking about. Stylistic considerations are useful but, as I have demonstrated, could be misleading. Epigraphic evidence is the least dependable because building inscriptions can readily be appended at a later date by a regime to wipe out the memory of a past history and substitute a new context. I am confident that additional, comprehensive, scientific dating will corroborate this hypothesis.

The failure of the standard paradigm has led me to seek answers that suggest roots for the three monuments that go back to Phoenicia. While admittedly the evidence is not incontrovertible, its very inadequacies are due in part to the fact that scholars have not been looking into this avenue of inquiry. When this new paradigm is considered worthy of further investigation, it will undoubtedly prove to be a catalyst that will lead various interrelated fields of inquiry to new insights. A multi-professional, coordinated, sustained and funded research is needed to carry forward Spanish Islamic archaeological studies and, for that matter, all Islamic historical studies to new heights of understanding.

Bibliography

Alomar, Mohammed Abdulrahman

Islamic Architecture, Ph.D dissertation, The Pennsyvania State University, 2000.

Antonova, K.

A History of India, Book 1, Progress Publishers, Moscow, 1979.

Aubet, Maria Eugenia

The Phoenicians and the West, Cambridge University Press, Cambridge, 1987.

Bargebuhr, Frederick P.

"The Alhambra Palace of the Eleventh Century," Journal of the Warbourg and Courtold Institutes, Vol. XIX, 1956, nos. 3-4, July to December.
The Alhambra, A Cycle of Studies on the Eleventh Century in Moorish Spain, Walter de Gruter & Co., Berlin, 1968.

Barrucand, Marianne and Bednorz, Achim

Moorish Architecture in Andalusia, Taschen, New York, 1992.

Behrens-Abousief, Doris

The Minarets of Cairo, The American University in Cairo Press, Cairo, 1985.

Bierling, Marilyn R. (editor)

The Phoenicians In Spain: An Archaeological Review of the Eigth-Sixth Centuries B.C.E., Eisenbrauns, Winona Lake, Indiana, 2002.

Bernal, Martin

    Black Athena, Rutgers Univerity Press, New Brunswick, NJ, Vol. I, 1987.

    Black Athena Writes Back, Duke University Press, Durham, North Carolina, 2001.

Bloom, Jonathan M.

    "*Five Fatimid Minarets in Upper Egypt*", JSAH XLIII: 162-167, May 1984.

    "*The Revival of Early Islamic Architecture by the Umayyads of Spain,*" The Medieval Mediterranean: Cross-Cultural Contacts, ed. M. Chiat and K. Ryerson, St. Cloud, Minnesota, 1988.

    Minaret: Symbol of Islam, Oxford University Press, London, 1989.

Brennan, Herbie

    The Atlantis Enigma, Berkley Books, New York, 2000.

    Memoirs,

Creswell, K.A.C.

    A Short Account of Early Muslim Architecture, Lebanon Book Shop, Beirut, 1968.

Cuneo, Paul

    "*Architecture*", in Arts of Cappadocia, ed. by Luciano Giovannini, Nagel Publishers, Geneva, 1971.

De Santillana, Georgio and Hertha Von Dechend

    Hamlet's Mill, David R. Godine, 1977.

Dewald, Ernest T.

    "*The Appearance of the Horseshoe Arch in Western Europe*", AJA, 1922, pp. 316-337.

Dodds, Jerrilyn D.

> Architecture and Ideology in Early Medieval Spain, Pennsylvania State Univ. Press, University Park, 1989.
> *"The Great Mosque of Cordoba,"* Al-Andalus: The Art of Islamic Spain, ed. Jerrilyn D. Dodds, New York, 1992, pp. 11-25.

Fernández-Puertas, Antonio

> The Alhambra, I, From the Ninth Century to Yusuf I (1354), London, 1997.
> *"Mezquita de Cordoba. Trazado Proporcional de Su Planta General (siglos VIII-X)"*, Archivo Español de Arte, v. 73, no. 291 (July/Sept. 2000), pp. 217-247.

Fisher, Robert E.

> Art of Tibet, Thames and Hudson, London, 1997.

Giminez, Felix Hernandez

> El Alminar de Abd Al-Rahman III en la Mezquita Mayor de Cordoba, Patronata de la Alhambra, Granada, 1975.

Gomez-Moreno, Manuel

> Ars Hispaniae, Vol. III, Editorial Plus-Ultra, Madrid, 1951.

Goodwin, Godfrey

> Islamic Spain, Penguin Books, England, 1991.

Grabar, Oleg

> The Alhambra, Harvard University Press, Cambridge, Massachusetts., 1978.
> *"Two Paradoxes in the Arts of the Spanish Peninsula,"* in The Legacy of Muslim Spain, ed. Salma Khadra Jayvusi, Leiden, 1992: pp. 583-91.
> *"Notes sur le mihrab de la Grande Mosquée de Cordoue,"* in Le Mihrab, ed. Alexandre Papadopoulo, Leiden, 1990, pp. 115-122.

Hancock, Graham

> The Sign and the Seal, Simon and Schuster, New York, 1992.
> Fingerprints of the Gods, Crown Trade Paperbacks, New York, 1995.

Hapgood, Charles

> Maps of the Ancient Sea Kings, Chilton Books, Philadelphia and New York, 1966; Turnstone Books, London, 1979.

Havel, E. B.

> The Ancient and Medieval Architecture of India, S. Chand & Co., (Pvt.) LTD, Ram Naga, New Delhi-55, first published 1915, reprinted 1972.

Hawkins, Gerald S.

> *Letter from Hawkins to Mills*, November 14, 1990.
> Stonehenge Decoded, Doubleday, 1965.

Heyerdahl, Thor

> The Ra Expeditions, BCA, London, 1972.

Hawkins, Gerald S.

> Beyond Stonehenge, Harper and Rowe, New York, 1973.

Irwin, Robert

> The Alhambra, Harvard University Press, Cambridge, Massachusetts, 2004.

Joseph, Frank

> The Destruction of Atlantis, Bear and Company, Rochester, Vermont, 2002.

Kondratov, Alexander

> The Riddles of Three Oceans, Progress Publishers, Moscow, 1974.

Khoury, Nuha

"*The meaning of the Great Mosque of Cordoba in the tenth century,*" Muqarnas 13, pp. 80-98.

King, David A.

"*Astronomical Alignments in Medieval Islamic Religious Architecture*", reprinted from Annals of the New York Academy of Sciences, 1982.
"*Faces of the Kaaba,*" the Sciences, Vol. 22, no. 5, May/June 1982.

Lambert, Élie

Études Medievales, Tome III, Privat-Didier, 1956.
«*L'Histoire de la grande-mosquée de Cordoue aux VIII et IX siècle d'après des textes inédits,*» Annals d'Institut d'études Orientales d'Alger 2 (1936): pp. 165-179.

Levi-Provençal, E.

"*Les Citations du Muqtabis d'Ibn Hayyan relqtives aux aggrandissements de la grande-mosquée de Cordoue au IX siècle* », Arabica! (1954): pp. 89-92.

Lillo, Mercedès

«*Le Mihrab dans l'Andalus*», Le Mihrab dans l'Architecture et la Religion Musulmanes, E. J. Brill, Leiden, 1988.

Lowney, Chris

A Vanished World: Medieval Spain's Golden Age of Enlightenment, Free Press, New York, 2005.

MacDonald, William

The Architecture of the Roman Empire, An Introductory Study, rev. ed., publications in the History of Art, no. 17, Yale University Press, 1982.

Marçais, George

"*Sur les mosaiques de la Grande Mosquée de Cordoue,*" Studies in Islamic Art and Architecture in Honour of K.A.C. Creswell, Cairo, 1965, pp. 147-156.

Menocal, María Rosa

The Ornament of the World, Little Brown and Co., Boston, 2002.

Mann, Vivian B. et al

Convivencia: Jews, Muslims and Christians in Medieval Spain, George Braziller, New York, 1992.

Mills, Marvin H.

"*Phoenician Origins of the Mosque of Cordoba, Madina Azahara and the Alhambra*", selected proceedings of the International Medieval Congress at the University of Leeds, 10-13 July 1995, 8-11 July 1996, Across the Mediterranean Frontiers: Trade, Politics and Religion, *650-1450*, ed. by D.A. Agius and I. R. Netton, Turnhout, Brepols, 1997.

"*The pre-Islamic provenance of the Mosque of Cordoba*", Al Masaq, Studia Arabo-Islamica, Mediterranea 4, 1991.

"*Scenario for a Roman Provenance for the Mosque of Cordoba*", The Medieval Mediterranean: Cross-Cultural Contacts, edited by M. J. Chiat and K. L. Reyerson, North Star Press of St. Cloud, Minnesota, 1988.

Moffitt, John F.

Art Forgery: The Case of the Lady of Elche, University Press of Florida, Gainseville, Florida, 1995.

Monco, Rafael

"*The Mosque and the Cathedral*", FMR: The Magazine of Franco Maria Ricci, 1988; pp. 98-117.

Narby, Jeremy Moscati

> The Cosmic Serpent, Jeremy P. Tarcher/Putnam, New York, 1999.

Nicolle, David

> The Mongol Warlords, Brockhampton Press, London, 1990.

Papadopoulu, Alexander

> *"Typologie des Mihrab"*, Le Mihrab dans l'Architecture et la Religion Musulmanes, A. Papadopoulu, E. J. Brill, Leiden, 1988; pp. 20-34.

Pym, Christopher

> The Ancient Civilization of Ankor, A Mentor Book, New, 1968.

Renfrew, Colin

> *"Ancient Europe is older than we thought"*, National Geographic, Nov. 1977, pp. 615-623.

Rivoira, G. T.

> Moslem Architecture, Hacker Art Books, New York, 1975.

Rodley, Lyn

> Cave Monasteries of Byzantine Cappadocia, Cambridge University Press, Cambridge, 1985.

Rodriguez, Dario Cabanelas

> *The Alhambra: an introduction*, in Al-Andalus—the Art of Islamic Spain, ed. by J. D. Dodds, New York, 1992, pp. 127-133.

Sauvaget, Jean

> La Mosquée Omeyyade de Medine, Paris, 1947.

Schoch, Robert M.

> Voyages of the Pyramid Builders, Jeremy P. Tarcher/Putnam, New York, 2003.

Stierlin, Henri and Anne

> Alhambra, Miroir de l'Univers, Imprimerie Nationale, Paris, 1991. *L'Alhambra: Jardins et bâtiments cosmiques sous les Nasrides, 1990.*

Terrasse, Henri

> L'Art Hispano-Mauresque des Origines au XIIe Siècle, Paris, Éditions G. Van Oest, MCMXXII, 1932.

Torres Balbas, L.

> La Mezquita de Cordoba y las Ruinas de Madinat al-Zahra, Editorial Plus-Ultra, Madrid, 1960.

Triano, Antonio Vallejo

> *"The Triumph of the Islamic State",* in Al-Andalus: The Art of Islamic Spain, ed. by Jerrilyn D. Dodds, The Metropolitan Museum of Art, New York, 1992.

Wilson, Colin and Flem-Ath, Rand

> The Atlantis Blueprint, Delacorte Press, New York, 2000.

Yule, Sir Henry (Translator and Editor)

> Book of Ser Marco Polo the Venetian Concerning the Kingdoms and Marvels of the East, Vol. II, third edition, revised, John Murray, London, 1929.

Zapp, Ivar and Erikson, George

> Atlantis in America, Adventures Unlimited Press, Kempton, Illinois, 1998.

Zimmer, Heinrich

> Myths and Symbols in Indian Art and Civilization, Harper Torchbooks, Harper and Rowe, New York, 1946.

978-0-595-42325-5
0-595-42325-6

Lightning Source UK Ltd.
Milton Keynes UK
UKOW05f1212101114

241387UK00001B/344/P